Et Tu, Carthago?

edited by

Jesse Johanning

Alyssa Miller

Benjamin Simington

Zachary Resch

2013

Carthage College

Kenosha, Wisconsin

Table of Contents

Painting Tragedy:
Comparing Imagery in Dante's *Inferno* and Rousseau's *Second Discourse*

Rachael Kimmerling

In Rousseau's *Second Discourse* and Dante's *Inferno* each author goes beyond simple ideas manifested in words by painting a poetic picture of a world in which the thoughts and states of mind about which they speak can be accessed. Each of these illustrations demonstrate a world accessible only to the imagination as opposed to tangible one that has been previously articulated through science, religion, or the popular views of society, making these images essential to the understanding of the concepts they help to guide.

From his very first lines Dante describes the Divine Comedy as a journey along which the reader must accompany him to fully comprehend. The fact that he plays two roles, representing both the poet and the pilgrim, demonstrates this. It is not enough to simply tell the story, but like Dante, one must travel with him and experience the *Inferno* as he does. Based on this idea of accompanying Dante on this journey as a pilgrim it is necessary for the reader to feel what he feels, as well as see all that he sees. Over the course of this journey one realizes that the people Dante encounters do not seem too displeased to find themselves in Hell, nor do they seem phased by the horrendous tortures they are forced to endure and will continue to endure for an eternity.

Rather, the Inferno's inhabitants continue to wallow in the same desires that they did in life remaining ever consumed by the sin that initially damned them. When Dante encounters his former teacher, Brunetto Latini, near the end of their discussion he says "Let my Tesoro, in which I still live, be precious to you; and I ask no more" (15:119-120). Even in death as he is suffering for his crime of sodomy, Brunetto is still obsessed by the false legacy he attempted to establish. Using these encounters as a guide it becomes obvious that this is not a place for those seeking to reform or even those who feel remorse for their sinning, as Dante describes that Brunetto "appeared to be the winner not the loser" (15:124). Therefore the circle in which each sinner dwells is not meant to serve as a punishment necessarily, but if anything a representation of how much their sin consumes them even after death. This idea that the sinner is depicted in a way that the punishment he or she receives coincides with the crime is a concept described as a *contre passo*. However, what Dante does takes it even a step further; not only does the punishment fit the crime, but serves as a representation that they live in sin eternally.

Looking at the world of the *Inferno* as a whole, Dante sets it up in a manner that is initially surprising. Despite his Christian background, the manner by which Dante constructs his idea of Hell does not seem in keeping with religious doctrine or even societal priority. In contrast with these social and religious dogmas, Dante's construction judges crimes based in reason with a heavier hand than those of mere physical action. More specifically, Dante places fraud, a crime committed solely through the abuse of reason, at a lower level than violence because in the hierarchy of human qualities reason resides at the top. To the top of the Inferno one would find crimes of flesh that can be seen as mere weaknesses rather than true exploitations such as gluttony and adultery. As one descends further into its depths there are more heinous crimes like fraud, which demand reason and planning, causing the overall exploitation of the soul. This corresponds with Rousseau's account of the natural man in which he presents the idea that passion is natural - for "[his] desires do not exceed his physical needs" (116)- and it is only through the development of reason that man deviates from this natural state, and in this new state man finds suffering consequential to knowledge and reason. To supplement this Rousseau states that "an animal will never know what it is to die; and knowledge of death and its terrors is one of the first acquisitions that man has made in moving away from the animal condition" (116). What Dante presents is the idea that the most highly revered desires are those that pursue beauty and knowledge, and it is through the success of these pursuits that allows for transcendence. Those that fall short of fulfilling these goals contort their result into something so perverse that it renders the seeker infernal. In contrast, Rousseau presents knowledge and beauty as unnatural desires and presents the highest pursuit as freedom, and to desire this is also rooted in the unnatural. In both cases the abuse of human reason is not only inevitable, but results negatively for the individual. The question of the possibility for human happiness through the ideas presented in these two works relates to Rousseau's statement of the inability to return to the happy natural states.

In the *Second Discourse*, Rousseau creates a demonstrative history of man claiming that "Everything that comes from nature will be true; there will be nothing false except what I have involuntarily put in on my own" (104). However, this statement coupled with the ideas Rousseau presents about how much of man remains natural and what artificial means have tainted him allows this statement to be read differently. If one uses Rousseau's logic it would be true that all that he contributes about man is in fact untrue, for his assertions are not derived from basic human needs for survival. Rousseau also makes other statements that are clearly contradictory which would make one question what he is truly trying to convey. For example, when he speaks of the Carib he says that he has no concept of the future through the reasoning that "in the morning he sells his bed of cotton and in the evening he comes weeping to buy it back, for want of having foreseen that he would need it for the coming night" (117). This of course if contradictory for the reason that if the Carib had no concept of the future, he would not think to sell a possession to earn money, which has no value except for what it can be traded for in the future. In addition to this, Rousseau also uses other absurd images to create transitions and explanations as to how certain stages of man developed. The image of an erupting volcano being the driving natural force that spurred the creation of metal ware seems completely arbitrary, and it is absurd conclusions such as this one about the development of various aspects of humankind that almost discredit the ideas Rousseau presents, especially considering his statement that "[it] is very difficult to guess how men came to know the use of iron" (152). This makes one question whether or not he has fully thought through the ideas he presents, and why he relies so heavily on what he does not know and he himself described as false. However, when one focuses on Rousseau's description of the most primitive state of man, it is difficult to even regard the being Rousseau describes as human at all. For example, it is not until after a few stages of advancement that people begin to live together. These odd and unprecedented suggestions about the so-called "natural" state of man juxtaposed with ridiculously far-fetched transitions create the possibility for an alternate meaning behind the ideas Rousseau presents. More specifically, it calls into question the idea that man may have once existed as a solely independent individual, that there was a time in which men did not band together, for to live socially is instinctual for many animals. Additionally, it also causes one see the potential for the "unnatural" changes that man experiences to actually be a representation of a process that was inevitable from the start, and since he asserts that only what is from nature is true, it makes one question everything he says about the unnatural state of man.

The fundamental difference between Dante and Rousseau is that their acknowledgement of a state of true paradise has its occurrence at completely different times of the state of being. Specifically, Dante describes how paradise is achievable at the end of the mortal life. "When she'd laid bare the truth of this poor life / Of miserable and mortal humankind, / She who exalts my mind to Paradise" (Paradiso 16:1-3). This acknowledgement of the inevitable misery of the mortal life demonstrates the tragic nature of the human life, but Dante offers a solution that can be realized through the imagination. In the same sense, Arthur Schopenhauer describes how this is something that each person must realize on their own as Dante does that "... the very best art is too spiritual to be given directly to the senses; it must be born in the beholder's imagination, though it must be begotten by the work of art. It is due to this that the sketches of great masters are often more effective than their finished paintings" (Schopenhauer 408), so to reach paradise one must supplement the masterpiece of life with their own images. Rousseau on the other hand presents paradise as an epoch of the past, impossible to return to as a result of the reason that has corrupted mankind. Additionally he offers no solution or possibility for transcendence. Despite this, if one contributes his or her own means it is possible to uncover possible solutions to this seemingly tragic world Rousseau presents.

Rousseau creates this idea that seems to point only in the direction of man's inevitable misery because of the impossibility of returning to the state of nature. However, beneath what seems like inescapable damnation by burden of knowledge lie a few possibilities for salvation. One solution can be seen through the qualms he seems to have with societal desires for power, which he expresses in saying that "citizens let themselves be carried away by blind ambition; and looking more below than above them" (Rousseau 173). Moreover, this statement demonstrates the problems in society that citizens seek recognition of their superiority. This seems to allude to the elimination of the class struggle in a communistic manner, but for someone who himself admits to the futility of trying to create a new government that people already corrupted by knowledge and the ability to compare could enjoy this does not seem like a serious option. Therefore, one is left to contemplate what could bring true happiness or at least as much happiness as is possible outside the natural state. "[The] sociable man, always outside of himself, knows how to live only in the opinion of others; and it is, so to speak, from their judgment alone that he draws the sentiment of his own existence" (Rousseau 179). If perhaps man could find a life that even when immersed in the opinions of others that he would not merely seek to be seen favorably in the eyes of his peers but to covet them in a way that could be channeled into a way of looking at the world. This philosophical path would allow one to use the human intellect in a purely contemplative manner. So therefore by looking at his portrayal of what at first seems to be a condemning flaw of the modern man, Rousseau shows through a sort of philosophical satire that reason and the social nature of man create the potential for happiness through philosophical means.

Dante's adaptation of his own representation of Hell demonstrates an entity that can be seen as his own philosophy on life that intertwines his views both as a Christian and as a member or society striving for the goodness of the world. Through his linguistically painted Inferno, he travels to the root of what he views as the greatest dangers to society through using the imagery of Hell as a necessary tool to communicate the degree of evil that each of these categories of people possess. In an equally effective use of illustration, Rousseau creates an original state of man that is so far removed from what man is actually thought of as being that one questions whether or not this state of nature ever could have been. This idea coupled with absurd images and stories display Rousseau's idea that once one looks at a more primitive state of living from the outside how absurd it seems that such a world could have ever once existed. Both Dante and Rousseau take on the role of linguistic artists by painting pictures with words that allow those who delve into their works of art to imagine a world that the artists themselves have created to demonstrate the opportunity for man's transcendence beyond the horrifying and often hopeless world in which he exists.

Works Cited

Alighieri, Dante. *Paradiso.* Trans. Anthony Esolen. Toronto: Random House, Inc, 2004.

Schopenhauer, Arthur. *The World as Will and Representation.* Vol. 2. Trans. E. F. J. Payne. New York: Dover Publications, Inc, 1958.

Shytonio: Similarities Between Shylock and Antonio that Demonstrate Christian Hypocrisy

Alyssa Scott

Since the play is named after him, Antonio becomes the central Christian and merchant figure present in The Merchant of Venice. He is beloved and respected by everyone as an honest and kind businessman who represents Christianity as a whole. As an assertion of his authority as a dominant and respected character, he speaks the first line of the play, "In sooth I know not why I am so sad" (1.1.1). Although his presentation as a fundamentally good character has truth, it is important to note that one character does hate him, Shylock, and the animosity is mutual. In this way, hatred serves as one of the many links between these two characters; after looking more closely at the occupations, private lives, and religiosity of both more similarities accrue. The height of the tension between these two characters occurs in the trial scene where the audience is left feeling that the dominant group in society—Antonio and the Christians—decides the administration of justice even though it might not really be fair.

Merchants and Money

According to his first line, the very first thing we learn about Antonio is that he is melancholy and does not know the reason. He goes even further to express his current feelings, saying that he does not really understand himself.

> But how I caught it, found it, or came by it,
> What stuff 'tis made of, whereof it is born,
> I am to learn;
> And such a want-wit sadness makes of me
> That I have much ado to know myself. (1.1.3-7)

Antonio's desire to acquire self-knowledge is a big part of this play, and also lets the audience "Assume that what Antonio is 'to learn'...must portend him ill" (Danson 41). All of these lines are end-stopped except the last two, indicating pauses and a thought process up until his final strong statement showing his anguish in this situation. Also, this speech is unique because it does not strictly follow iambic pentameter; line three is one syllable too long and line five is six syllables too short. Straying from the norm in this manner goes even further to show Antonio's mental anguish, which other characters in his presence pick up on. Salerio and Salanio guess that he is either worried about losing money with the latest merchandise he purchased or is preoccupied by something to do with love. Both are reasonable conclusions, but Antonio denies them.

Peculiarly enough, another friend suggests for a second time that worrying about money makes Antonio sad. Gratiano says to him, "You have too much respect upon the world; / They lose it that do buy it much with care" (1.1.74-75). Gratiano hints that Antonio regards the world highly and he does so because he buys his regard, meaning he is materialistic. Following this idea, David Nirenberg paraphrases the two passages and suggests Antonio's concern with the ships bearing his merchandise: "You think of nothing but your money. Everything else, no matter how sacred, reminds you only that your investments are at risk" (81). Later in the play Antonio condemns Shylock for this same attitude towards money. Since both Gratiano and Salerio think that Antonio is worried about the same thing, it seems plausible that it be true.

However, Gratiano's words are not the last on this subject. Antonio responds to Gratiano's statement of his character, "I hold the world but as the world Gratiano— / A stage, where every man must play a part, / And mine a sad one" (1.1.77-79). This comment implies acceptance of his sadness as part of his trade, one where he constantly risks losing things. The nature of his job being insecure and making money without really benefitting anyone could also attribute to his melancholy. Everyone in Venice has great respect for Antonio and thinks highly of him. Therefore, the audience hears a lot of praise for him including Solanio saying, "The good Antonio, the honest Antonio—O that I had a title good enough to keep his name company!" (3.1.12-14). The fact that his trade is not a very noble one, certainly less noble than something such as a doctor or a judge, seems to cause him guilt for his lack of doing good in the world as Christians are taught.

If Antonio is the star of this play, then the character of Shylock is the antagonist who mirrors Antonio in many ways. It is commonly believed that he is no more than a villain who has a plan and tries to kill Antonio. However, as Stephen Greenblatt points out, if this were Shakespeare's intention for the character of

Shylock he could and would have made it more obvious. "In the late sixteenth century it would certainly have been possible for Shakespeare to exploit such lurid stories...but he chose not to do so" (Greenblatt 57). The lurid stories are those of Jews murdering Christians to consume the blood in preparation for their holidays along with others of the same nature, which can also be found in Christopher Marlowe's contemporary play The Jew of Malta. If such a depiction of the Jewish Shylock had been chosen by Shakespeare, there would have been no doubt as to his being a villain, but that is not the case. On the contrary, what may seem villainous in the character of Shylock is directly parallel to Antonio's character.

Similar to Antonio's introduction, we learn about Shylock's occupation first. He first appears in the midst of making a deal with Bassanio. Like Antonio, work is very important to Shylock and the first thing we learn about him is his occupation as a moneylender. His first line, "Three thousand ducats—well" (1.3.1) identifies him as a businessman and implies that his occupation is very important to him. Throughout the beginning of this scene, we see Shylock as a very methodical and thoughtful character; he repeats what Bassanio tells him about the loan, usually adding a "well" to the end of it to show his consideration of what is being said. Anita Gilman Sherman's interpretation agrees with this, "Shylock's first words—phrases broken up by a set of 'well's show him sizing up a situation and ruminating" (279). Therefore he takes business seriously and makes it an important part of his life.

The malaise of Antonio is most likely a result of the lack of Christian ethics in his trade, and this could be a reason why he values Bassanio and his relationship with him so highly. By being generous, giving, and selfless towards Bassanio he makes up for the unethical nature of his work. Lawrence Danson agrees with this reading of Antonio's occupation and mentions that most Elizabethans seeing this play performed would have been wary of Antonio as a profit-making merchant; they might feel admiration, jealousy, and even moral disapproval towards him (25). The moral disapproval of Antonio would come from the fact that merchants made their fortunes "Less through the sweat of their brow than through the manipulation of money itself" (Danson 26). Accordingly, most sixteenth century viewers of this play would pick up on this capitalistic tendency of Antonio's to love money and make a connection to Shylock's greed that is not immediately apparent to twenty-first century readers or viewers.

Shylock also earns money without having to labor. The one difference between the practices of these two men is that Shylock's loans are given with interest attached, whereas Antonio believes this to be a horrid practice. Usury, according to Christianity, had been a crime in the past. Even though at the time this play was written usury was legal, it was still controversial and many people disapproved of it. However, in his dealing with a Christian that so greatly disliked this practice Shylock was not willing to make an exception. Shylock asks Antonio, "Methoughts you said you neither lend nor borrow upon advantage" (1.3.66-67) making it clear he has the power in this business transaction and is not going to follow Antonio's ideals just to make one deal. He also directly addresses the fact that Antonio has condemned his practices, "Signior Antonio, many a time and oft / In the Rialto you have rated me / About my moneys and my usances" (1.3.103-105). Not only does this make Shylock a character that the audience is skeptical of, but Antonio even more so. Bringing up his criticism of Shylock along with the fact that Antonio has declared he will never borrow or lend money with interest makes both characters equally morally repugnant. Shylock is condemned for being a usurer, but now Antonio is also dealing in usury.

The Private Lives of Antonio and Shylock

After learning about Antonio's occupation, we are introduced to his personal life and his great love for Bassanio. The second suggestion for why Antonio is so sad is that he is in love. Antonio denies this, but we soon learn that he would do anything for his friend Bassanio. We are first introduced to Bassanio as if he is a family member of Antonio's when Solanio says, "Here comes Bassanio, your most noble kinsman" (1.1.57). When Bassanio begins to speak, he tells Antonio about a woman he wishes to marry, Portia, but he has no money to make the voyage to Belmont. Part of Antonio's response is, "Within the eye of my honor, be assured/My purse, my person, my extremest means/Lie all unlocked to your occasions" (1.1.137-139). From this it is evident that Antonio will do anything for Bassanio; his love goes so far that he is willing to get a loan from Shylock so his friend can travel to Belmont. Then, Bassanio uses this implied family connection to his advantage when he says "I urge this childhood proof / Because what follows is pure innocence" (1.1.143-144). This way he makes his proposal for money seem as though it is coming from "The need of a very young dependent [on Antonio]" (Penuel 260). With this statement we see the implied familial connection is approved and used by both characters.

Antonio acts more like a father or godfather figure to Bassanio. He is unfailingly generous in regards to his friend because his happiness is derived from Bassanio's happiness. Antonio is, according to critic W. Thomas MacCary, "An older, weaker, sentimental male protector, a father without a father's authority or a father's demand for love and obedience" (168). So Bassanio seems to both solve and perpetuate Antonio's problem of being sad; he is happy when Bassanio is happy, but by giving Bassanio money to get married he will in a sense lose his friend to Portia.

This potential sadness at the idea of losing something so important to him mirrors Shylock's reaction when he finds out that his daughter has fled and sold one of his rings. Since Bassanio is the only person close to Antonio that we are introduced to, Bassanio serves as the equivalent of Jessica to Shylock. Not only is Shylock hated by Antonio, but his own daughter Jessica even says, "Our house is hell" (2.3.2) when talking to their servant Launcelot who has decided to work elsewhere. The conflicts created by Launcelot and Jessica show us that Shylock has some difficulty in his personal life, just as Antonio does in having to let go of his friend Bassanio with his pending marriage.

First, we see Launcelot convince Bassanio to take him on as a servant so he can escape the house of Shylock. "To be brief, the very truth is that the Jew, having done me wrong doth cause me..." (2.2.131-132), says Launcelot in his appeal to Bassanio. However, Launcelot is not a reliable source to learn about the character of Shylock since his introduction in the stage directions is Launcelot the clown. We also learn of Jessica's predicament with wanting to marry the Christian Lorenzo and her father's inevitable disapproval. Although juvenile, her frustration is understandable since he is threatening to get in the way of her happiness. In these scenes where Jessica and Launcelot complain about Shylock's unfair treatment towards them, it is important to note Shylock's lack of presence, which represents his distance from these characters in a much larger sense. When other characters talk about him they portray him as purely evil. However, when Shylock is actually on stage his humanity and vulnerability become clear (Lyon 62). One great example of this more human side of Shylock can be seen on the Rialto when he asks people for information about his daughter.

In this scene some of Shylock's more memorable lines are given about his realization that Jessica ran off with some valuable possessions. He seems torn between mourning his daughter and his lost treasure as Salanio retells the story, "I never heard a passion so confused...'My daughter! O my ducats! O my daughter!...Justice! The law! My ducats and my daughter!" (2.8.12-17). Seemingly significant is that Shylock feels conflicted about what matters more to him, his ducats or his daughter, and then in his final statement ducats is said before daughter showing his decision. More important to note is that the audience hears all this secondhand, creating a distance from Shylock yet again. Lyon agrees about the importance of the nature of Shylock's reaction, "We are told of it rather than shown it, and told in terms of bawdy and satirical comedy" (63). Salanio's speech is quite lengthy and clearly means to poke fun at Shylock the Jew, calling him a dog and repeating daughter and ducats as many times as possible. So it can be concluded that he exaggerates the story and may even be lying.

Once Shylock appears onstage for the first time after Jessica flees, he confronts Salanio about his knowledge of Jessica's situation and has to deal with the jokes and insults of the other men. Then Tubal shows up and tells Shylock more about his daughter, including a ring she sold. Shylock responds, "Thou torturest me, Tubal... I had it of Leah when I was a bachelor. I would not have given it for a wilderness of monkeys" (3.2.113-116). Leah is his late wife and he valued her ring more than his lost money. Therefore, the tone of his response is one of grief. After hearing this, he starts out being angry and uses an exclamation point after his first statement to show it. Then he becomes more subdued and says this fact tortures him—admitting its value and that he would not have traded it for anything. He not only despairs for the loss of this ring, but for the knowledge that his daughter never understood the value of it. "At this moment Shylock discovers that Jessica has never understood the sentimental value that he attached to that ring and, worse still, that he has evidently failed to communicate and instill in her any attachment to the past" (Sherman 281). This reading provides more depth to Shylock's character as well as showing another similarity between him and Antonio. The audience here sees Shylock's capacity for love and his identification with something other than business. He values and loves his wife and his past as much as Antonio does his relationship with Bassanio.

Hatred and Religious Nature

Although Antonio comes across as a fundamentally good character, his representation of Christianity becomes more problematic the next time he appears in the middle of making a deal with Shylock for Bassanio's loan. If Antonio was courteous, gracious, and kind before, he is now the opposite. Cold and harsh could be added to his list of characteristics upon discovering from Shylock that Antonio has yelled at him, called him names, and spat on him. Antonio responds to Shylock, "I am as like to call thee so again, / To spet on thee again, to spurn thee too" (1.3.127-128). This is completely opposite of what we have seen and heard of Antonio up to this point, and he acts out of the same hate that we see Shylock has for Antonio.

Not only does he illustrate his hatred for Shylock, but his behavior is very unchristian. He shows no respect to Shylock, even calling him a devil that quotes Scripture. Antonio directly contradicts the Christian teaching to love your enemies since he treats Shylock as his enemy throughout this entire scene, and even admits his enmity towards Shylock. When asking for the loan, Antonio declares they are not friends and instead asks him, "But lend it rather to thine enemy" (1.3.132). Therefore, Antonio is "presumptuous of [his] goodness and righteousness [as a Christian]" (Hassel 180). His presumptuousness leads him to be self-righteous as well, which is similar to how Shylock later acts in the trial scene with his pursuance of the bond he made with Bassanio and Antonio. It is his presumptuousness and self-righteousness that serve as flaws to his character and create a conflict he faces as a protagonist. Accordingly, critic Craig Bernthal states his dilemma succinctly that "Antonio...has much to learn about forgiveness" (98) and after evaluating the trial scene we learn whether he does or does not.

Similarly, what makes Shylock seem most like a villain is his hatred for Antonio, and particularly his soliloquy that appears when making the deal with Bassanio and Antonio.

> "I hate him for he is a Christian;
> But more, for that in low simplicity
> He lends out money gratis, and brings down
> The rate of usance here with us in Venice.

> If I can catch him once upon the hip,
> I will feed fat the ancient grudge I bear him." (1.3.39-44)

While he does create the idea that he and Antonio are enemies, Shylock does not say anything derogative about the character of Antonio. Stoll says of this passage, "That a sleepy audience may not make the mistake...and take the villain for the hero, Shakespeare is at pains to label the villain by an aside at the moment the hero appears on the boards" (122). This speech begs the question of why Shylock has such a grudge against Antonio. One reason he gives is Antonio bringing down the interest rate in the economy of Venice by giving away loans, which decreases Shylock's income. However, it seems as though something else lurks under the surface of this speech and the very character of Shylock. Something important to notice about Shylock's speeches is the difference in when he uses prose and verse. At the beginning of his first scene, where the business transaction takes place, he speaks in prose. This shows his methodical nature and his evaluation of the loan. Once Antonio enters, he switches to verse—even in his aside quoted above. This indicates some underlying reason for Shylock's behavior.

An idea of Shylock's motivation as a character can be drawn from this habit of his speech, and his very nature. Critic Sherman addresses this motivation as well as what it has to do with the depth of his character, saying that in order to account for his behavior "it is necessary to understand him as a skeptic who cannot bear to acknowledge the failures of his knowledge"

(Sherman 277). Sherman presents Shylock as a character who has two main flaws: being a skeptic and not being able to acknowledge his own failures. This inability to acknowledge failures is what makes him so obsessed with money; it is his escape from the reality of his life. This is very similar to Antonio's obsession with doing everything he possibly can to make Bassanio happy as a way to make up for how he earns his living. His use of verse in front of other characters shows his guardedness and unwillingness to open himself up to people. Accordingly, Shylock rarely shows his softer side—only doing so because he feels despair at the idea of losing both his daughter and valuable memories of the past. Since his sentimentality has worked against him in this case with his daughter, he seeks revenge on the only other place he has shown emotion, although it was hatred, and we are thus led to the trial scene where he adamantly seeks one pound of Antonio's flesh.

Justice and the Trial

At the beginning of the trial to determine if Shylock can extract a pound of Antonio's flesh, the tone immediately elicits pity for Antonio's situation. This becomes clear when the Duke says, "I am sorry for thee. Thou art come to answer / A stony adversary, an inhuman wretch, / Uncapable of pity" (4.1.3-5). His lines also set Shylock apart as Antonio's opposite—cruel, unjust, and merciless.

Following this introduction, Antonio becomes a Christ-like figure. Whenever Antonio speaks of Shylock in prior scenes, he always uses strong, harsh, and loud words. Now he becomes more subdued and resigned to his fate saying he is prepared "To suffer with a quietness of spirit / The very tyranny and rage of his" (4.1.12-13). Not only has his tone changed, but his attitude as well. Antonio usually takes every opportunity to argue with Shylock and point out his inferiority, but now he resigns himself to the will of Shylock. Before the audience can feel too much pity for Antonio, the reason Antonio finds himself in this situation must be recalled. He has behaved in a very unchristian manner in his treatment of Shylock—"You call me misbeliever, cutthroat dog, / And spet upon my Jewish gaberdine" (1.3.108-109) Shylock comments. Remembering his former cruelty helps dispel the idea that Antonio parallels Christ during the trial.

As the scene continues, Antonio remains submissive to Shylock's will. When Portia asks if he has anything to say about the absence of a doctor to attend to him if Shylock cuts too deep he responds, "But little" (4.1.263). He then holds Bassanio's hand and speaks with him.

> "Grieve not that I am fall'n to this for you,
> For herein Fortune shows herself more kind
> Than is her custom: it is still her use
> To let the wretched man outlive his wealth." (4.1.265-268)

Along with his other speeches in the first half of this scene, this one is slow-moving and has a tone of helplessness. He claims to be at the mercy of Fate; there is nothing he can do so he gives up without a fight. He also makes himself into a martyr or sacrifice—

his life for Bassanio's happiness. This not only gives Shylock an upper hand obtaining his pound of flesh, but also moral superiority for the time being. Antonio admits he is a "wretched man" lucky to be dying rather than living and dealing with the consequences of his actions and behaviors. Implicitly, he sees the error of his ways as a Christian, either in his occupation or his treatment of Shylock, and accepts punishment for it.

On the other hand, Shylock is portrayed in the complete opposite light; to a person who failed to notice the pain he endured when Jessica left, he seems bloodthirsty and determined to get revenge. His obsession with the bond has a connection to the failure he feels as a result of Jessica leaving in the manner she did, and he pursues the bond so persistently because he cannot bear another failure. Evidence of this can be seen by his attitude— he goes back to being his closed-off and removed self. He keeps distance from the scene at hand, the characters in it, and even the audience when he turns down multiple opportunities to accept monetary payment for his bond instead.

> "You'll ask me why I rather choose to have
> A weight of carrion flesh than to receive
> Three thousand ducats. I'll not answer that,
> But say it is my humor." (4.1.40-43)

He not only refuses Antonio's money, but also refuses to say why he will not accept it; he does not tell us that he feels like a failure because he is too proud and afraid of the possible catastrophe another failure would cause.

Even though Shylock and Antonio act completely different from one another, they do so for similar reasons—they both feel they have failed in some respect. The similarity between these two is evident when Portia enters the scene and has to ask who is who. "I am informed thoroughly of the case. / Which is the merchant here? And which the Jew?" (4.1.172-173) Portia asks. She does not find out until she asks a second time after being presented with them both if Shylock is in fact Shylock.

Upon Portia's entrance, a new concept is introduced to the scene—Christian mercy. She continually asks Shylock to be merciful, even when she has granted him the right to extract a pound of Antonio's flesh. This seems to be a test, and one that Shylock fails because he shows no sign of mercy and immediately prepares to extract the pound of flesh. Once Shylock makes it clear he has no intention of being merciful, Portia switches tactics and reads the bond even more literally than Shylock. As the tables have turned, Shylock learns that if Antonio bleeds it will be taken as an intention to kill Antonio. Because of his Jewish faith, Shylock is perceived as an alien. Thus, in seeking the life of a citizen, Antonio, more punishment will come his way if he acts on the bond.

> "The party 'gainst the which he doth contrive
> Shall seize one half his goods; the other half
> Comes to the privy coffer of the state;
> And the offender's life lies in the mercy
> Of the Duke only." (4.1.351-355)

At this point, Shylock realizes he has lost and been disgraced. Half of his worldly possessions will go to Antonio and the other half to the government of Venice. His response to this shows him at his most vulnerable point, "Nay, take my life and all! Pardon not that!...You take my life / When you do take the means whereby I live" (4.1.373-376). He now begs for the mercy that Portia attempted to persuade him to give earlier, but he does not receive it. Instead, as well as taking most of his possessions they also force him to convert to Christianity. As Christians they should have extended the mercy they originally asked for. On the contrary, they did worse than simply following the law in how they chose to punish him.

The outcome of the trial becomes especially problematic when put in context with the character of Antonio who represents Christianity as a whole. While he thought he was doomed he forgave Shylock for pursuing the bond and accepted his punishment. Once it becomes clear he has power again he changes and goes back to his former treatment of Shylock. Portia gives him the opportunity to render mercy unto Shylock and at first it seems he might. He begins by asking the duke not to demand half of his worth and instead give it to his daughter as well as asking "That for his favor / He presently become a Christian" (4.1.385-386). If he had truly forgiven Shylock like a good Christian ought to, he would have defended Shylock and prevented his complete humiliation in being forced to convert.

Rather, he is the one that asks for this humiliation to be brought upon Shylock.

Shylock also receives different treatment in this scene than most Shakespearean villains; when they are coming undone all of them are given exit lines and have a last word. For example, in the final scene of Othello after Iago's plot has been exposed his last lines are, "Demand me nothing. What you know, you know. / From this time forth I never will speak word" (Othello, 5.2.308-309). Even though Iago clearly does not have a chance of getting off clean, he still retains power in his last lines because he refuses to speak before being brought offstage. However, Shylock is not given such a powerful exit line. Instead, he begs after his conversion, "I pray you give me leave to go from hence. / I am not well" (4.1.394-395). Then immediately after Gratiano expresses his opinion on what Shylock's punishment should have been, we see in the stage direction that Shylock exits. The result of the trial, as Nirenberg concludes as well, shows that the "Christian mercies"—the confiscation of his possessions and Shylock's choice between death or converting to Christianity—end up being just as, if not more, cruel than everyone condemned Shylock of being in the beginning (96).

By the end of the trial Antonio comes out the winner, but Shylock comes out the moral superior of the two. As the similarities between their occupations and dealings with money, their private lives, and the reflection of their behavior on their respective religions have shown, throughout most of the play they are moral equals. However, during the trial Antonio has the opportunity to be a good Christian and rise above Shylock but he does not. He has the power to deny taking half of Shylock's worldly possessions and refusing to allow a conversion to take place by fully forgiving Shylock for his actions. Also, Shylock's decision not to kill Antonio but rather to suffer his punishment of having everything, including his Jewish identity, taken from him instead of choosing the easy way out with his own death makes him morally superior. Another example of his morality comes from comparing a statement Shylock made at the beginning of the trial with his later actions. "Hates any man the thing he would not kill?" (4.1.67) he asks. Since he could not actually kill Antonio, he suggests he no longer hates Antonio and therefore acknowledges the wrong of his previous hateful actions. On the other hand, Antonio does not practice the mercy that he and other Christians preach—thereby showing a great example of Christian hypocrisy. The dominant group in society, the Christians, decided Justice in this trial. Although the results were unfair, they reveal a truth about society that only members of lesser groups need to change because the dominant group is always right, and any others are always wrong.

Works Cited

Bernthal, Craig. *The Trial of Man: Christianity and Judgment in the World of Shakespeare.* Wilmington: ISI Books, 2003. Print.

Danson, Lawrence. *The Harmonies of* The Merchant of Venice. New York: Yale University Press, 1978. Print.

Greenblatt, Stephen. *Shakespeare's Freedom*. Chicago: The University of Chicago Press, 2010. Print.

Hassel, R. Chris, Jr. *Faith and Folly in Shakespeare's Romantic Comedies*. Athens: The University of Georgia Press, 1980. Print.

Lyon, John. *Twayne's New Critical Introductions to Shakespeare*: The Merchant of Venice. Boston: Twayne Publishers, 1988. Print.

MacCary, W. Thomas. *Friends and Lovers: The Phenomenology of Desire in Shakespearean Comedy*. New York: Columbia University Press, 1985. Print.

Nirenberg, David. "Shakespeare's Jewish Questions." *Renaissance Drama*, New Series 38 (2010): 77-113. Project Muse. Web. 10 April 2012.

Penuel, Suzanne. "Castrating the Creditor in "The Merchant of Venice." *Studies in English Literature*, 1500-1900 44.2 (2004): 255-275. JSTOR. Web. 10 April 2012.

Sherman, Anita Gilman. "Disowning Knowledge of Jessica, or Shylock's Skepticism." *Studies in English Literature*, 1500-1900 44.2 (2004):277-295. JSTOR. Web. 10 April 2012.

Stoll, Elmer Edgar. *Shakespeare Studies*. New York: The Macmillan Company, 1927. Print.

The Shortcoming of a Great American: Benjamin Franklin and Humility

Zachary Resch

In his autobiography, Benjamin Franklin gathered together a list of thirteen virtues that he deemed necessary or desirable. The last among these was the virtue of humility to which he attached the precept "Imitate Socrates and Jesus" (*Autobiography*, 84). This virtue was the one that Franklin deemed the least attainable for himself, possibly for all humanity, because he says that the list was created in a way that the acquisition of the previous virtues would facilitate the mastering of the later virtues. Through the positioning of humility in the ultimate position upon the list, Franklin indicates that all virtues preceding would have been mastered before the acquisition of humility could have been attempted in a way for that virtue to be firmly grounded. The task at hand presents us with the need to explicate the virtue of humility, but one must understand that this requires examining humility's twofold-nature. The two components of humility presented by Franklin are "the imitation of Socrates" and "the imitation of Jesus Christ." The preliminary investigation of humility will be set forth by showing the constitution of the two components, namely "the imitation of Socrates" and "the imitation of Christ," and then showing how humility arises from bringing these components together.

The precept of imitating Socrates can be approached from the different perspectives that lay dependent on how one views the life of this philosopher. The only clarity in characterizing the life of Socrates is that there is a lack of clarity due to Socrates not having produced written work of his own. Therefore, we necessarily have to rely on the accounts of those who were present during the life of Socrates and find the virtue of his life through their interpretations. But how are we to know what to accept as true when there has been controversy in the interpretation of Socrates' life since before his death? Is the great comic Aristophanes' account any less credible than that of Socrates' pupils Plato or Xenophon? The answer is that in our investigation, one will have to examine which interpretation was embraced by Franklin. In light of Franklin's claims to have picked up "the Socratic Method" from reading the *Memorable Things of Socrates* by another of Socrates' pupils, Xenophon, we may suggest the likelihood that the approach of the life of Socrates was Platonic in manner. Socrates, as a character of Plato, was said to possess wisdom because of his acknowledgment of self-ignorance and ignorance of the world, which Plato amply has the character Socrates acknowledge, "ὃς οὐδέν φημι ἄλλο ἐπίστασθαι ἢ τὰ ἐρωτικά" [as I claim to have expert knowledge of nothing but erotics] (*Symposium*, 177E); even this little knowledge was taught to him by Diotima. The description of Socrates' life can be further understood when one examines the method of inquiry used by the wandering philosopher Socrates during his examination of such things as piety, love, etc. The character

Socrates was often described as philosophizing in an impoverished condition because contemplating the right way to live was seen as a greater pursuit than wealth or honor, which would have ended this poverty. Here, one can see that the humility of Socrates takes on a dual significance: through the claim of being ignorant and through living in poverty, both for the sake of a purer pursuit of knowledge. In accepting this elucidation of the Platonic Socrates as an exemplar of the virtue of humility, Benjamin Franklin's actualization of imitating Socrates to gain humility can be said to be mere semblance. One of the only recordings of Franklin's own imitation of Socrates was when he adopted the Socratic method and "took a Delight in it, practis'd it continually & grew very artful & expert in drawing People even of superior Knowledge into Concessions the Consequence of which they did not foresee, entangling them in Difficulties out of which they could not extricate themselves, and so obtaining Victories that neither myself nor my Cause always deserved" (*Autobiography*, 17). The imitation in the earliest attempts can be conceived to feed the vanity of Franklin rather than express his humility, for which he had donned the role of "the humble Inquirer & Doubter" (*Autobiography*, 16). The failed attempt at imitating Socrates may be a result of the unattainableness of the virtue of humility without first attaining the preceding virtues, especially silence and sincerity. We can examine the imitation of Jesus as the second component of the precept based on an essay concerning Christ written by Franklin on March 9, 1790. "As to Jesus of Nazareth ... I think the

System of Morals and his Religion, as he left them to us, the best the World ever saw or is likely to see" (*Autobiography*, 324). How does one suggest this brief statement reflects greatly on Franklin's opinion of Christ? And why, in a letter that asserts to share his opinion on Jesus, does the greater content reflect personal faith or the corruption of the Christian tradition? We can apprehend the content as such if we further question Franklin's doubt to the divinity of Jesus. Assuming the mortality of Jesus, Franklin beholds the Son of Man as a mere moral figure. Further, as a mortal, Jesus' own humility can be challenged based on the belief that corrupting changes, as to the nature of his life, were made by the Church to incorporate Christ into the godhead. The rejection of imitating Christ as a standard of humility appears to be additionally reflected in Franklin's response to a preacher's gratitude that an offer was made for Christ's sake, which Franklin viewed as shifting "the Burden of Obligation from off the [Saint's] own Shoulders, and [placing] it in Heaven" (*Autobiography*, 108). The moralistic "shifting of obligation" by the Saints, which was often done in imitation of Jesus, is a more humble manner of behavior because one does so, not to dissolve responsibility, but to avoid being vain in taking more credit than that which is due.

In gathering together the two components of humility, the imitation of Socrates on the one hand and the imitation of Jesus on the other, we are left with a rejection of the latter and an acceptance of the former as a mere belief. The conception of the mere belief comes into existence because Franklin never acted in a manner where one would think he sincerely imitated Socrates to become humble. Besides the notion of the difficulty of humility's attainability, there was the clear embrace of the contrary by Franklin when he expressed to his son that it is good to gratify one's vanity "being persuaded that it is often productive of Good to the Possessor & to others that are within his Sphere of Action" (*Autobiography*, 4). The Qur'an favors the humility that may arise in some when it calls on the Prophet to "give good news to the humble whose hearts fill with awe whenever God is mentioned, who endure whatever happens to them with patience, who keep up the prayer, who give to others out of Our provision to them" (*The Pilgrimage*). A person may seek the virtue of humility in such a way by strict religious devotion and good works, which can carry over into other religions such as Christianity. In a more extreme interpretation of humility, the Catholic theologian Meister Eckhart called for a renunciation of the self as the most sure humility and embracement of the divine, when he said, "Those who seek peace in external things, whether in places or devotional practices, people or works, in withdrawal from the world or poverty or self-abasement: however great these things may be or whatever their character, they are still nothing at all and cannot be the source of peace" (*The Talks of Instruction*). Regardless as to how one strictly interprets humility, there appears to be an inherent difficulty in the attainment of this virtue. So why should we endure the internal turmoil that emerges from the rigorousness of the pursuit that will overcome many, even of excellent moral stature, and appears to be infinite, as the furthest reaches cause us to renounce our identities? Is it that the pursuit of this virtue will instill other virtues in our being and, further, test our own endurance to aspire to the limits of human potential?

Naturally Endowed Misery

Hunter Sandidge

"It is not without difficulty that we have succeeded in making ourselves so [miserable]...However, man is naturally good" (193). Rousseau makes a profound claim that man, by nature, is good and has made himself miserable only through unnatural means. However, if one truly analyzes Rousseau's *Second Discourse*, he would find that this claim may be undermined by an even more profound and unfortunate reality: humanity by its very nature, and not necessarily or solely due to its own choices and volitions, was doomed, from whatever beginning there may have been, to live in the general condition of misery. Within the *Second Discourse*, Rousseau makes three claims to what are the distinctive capacities of humanity, from which all other capacities arise, excluding the fundamental faculties that form the base of all beasts. If one accepts those premises to be true, he will find that those qualities gave rise to man's present faculties, which are, according to Rousseau, the artificial means to and source of his misery.

Rousseau defines misery as, "...a word that...signifies a painful privation and the suffering of the body or soul" (127). In addition, Rousseau later goes on to describe how the lack of an unfulfilled, even inessential desire creates a type of suffering (147). Rousseau also provided examples to clarify what he meant by 'suffering of the soul':

"...excess of idleness in some, excess of labor in others; the ease of stimulating and satisfying our appetites and our sensuality; the overly refined foods of the rich...the bad food of the poor...late nights, excesses of all kinds, immoderate ecstasies of all the passions, fatigues and exhaustion of the mind; numberless sorrows and afflictions which are felt in all conditions and by which souls are perpetually tormented" (109-110).

It must be said that Rousseau's claim is that the *general* condition of man is that of misery. However, that is not to say that happiness does not exist, as he did provide examples of happiness within modern humanity (151,175). With misery defined, one can proceed to analyze Rousseau's three claims to the distinctive human qualities, observe the progression of these qualities to form new faculties, and also observe the rise of misery.

The first natural and distinctive human capacity, according to Rousseau, is man's ability to resist the 'rules of nature', being defined as those fundamental faculties that form the base of all living creatures: "...the distinction of man among animals...is his being a free agent...he realizes that he is free to acquiesce or resist [the rules of nature]" (114). Essentially, Rousseau makes the distinction that animals, "...cannot deviate from the rule that is prescribed to [them]" by nature, whereas man has the ability to defy and act against those rules (113). Rousseau provided an example of a cat starving surrounded by fruit: it could survive off the food, but by nature does not have the ability to make the choice to consume it, whereas in a similar situation, man would be able to make a decision that defies this general rule of nature, even if he disdains the option (114). However, it is important to make the distinction that man can resist the rules and fundamental capacities bestowed upon all animals, but not his own distinctive human nature, as man would not be able to resist his ability to choose, as that in itself would be a choice. Essentially, man's freedom extends only as far as he is unchained to the general rules of nature. Also, it is important to note the relationship between man being a free agent and the naturally endowed virtue, to all beasts, of pity: "...the innate repugnance to see his fellow man suffer" (130). Because man can resist the fundamental capacities, he has the *ability* (and not yet desire) to, voluntarily, make his brethren suffer by his own hand. Man's ability to contradict the rules of nature becomes of importance in combination with the other two distinctive human capacities and the subsequent progression of faculties that derive from them, as it is the platform from which misery arises. With this said, one can begin to assess the second uniquely human capacity.

The second exclusive faculty that Rousseau attributes to mankind is what he called 'perfectibility': "...this distinctive and almost unlimited faculty... [brings] to flower over the centuries his enlightenment..." (115). Essentially, it is this perfectibility that allowed man to excel and progress, compared to beasts which "...[are] at the end of a few months what [they] will be all [their] lives" (114-115). Perfectibility separates man from beast in the sense that it allows man to change and improve his capacities, yet in combination with the first distinctive human capacity, also allows man to ultimately corrupt himself. Perfectibility gave man enlightenment, which is later indirectly defined as the ability to contemplate or reason, though it is then important to note that perfectibility is described as an '*almost* unlimited faculty', which implies that man cannot achieve complete enlightenment (146). According to Rousseau, man was not initially given the ability to perceive the future, as, for early man, "His soul...is given over to the sole sentiment of its present existence without any idea of the future..." (117). Enlightenment then had to have given rise to foresight. For example, say a man, who had been attacked by bears in the past, was attacked by another, and on this occasion, he grabbed a large stick and beat off the bear. It is only from his ability to reason that, if he had been attacked in the past, and the stick made his defense much easier, he would realize it was likely for him to be attacked in the future, thus he should carry the stick with him, giving rise to the faculty of foresight. With knowledge of these faculties, being raised from perfectibility, one can then assess the final distinctive human capacity.

The final unique faculty of man is that of self-perception: "...there is another very specific quality that distinguishes [man and beast] and about which there can be no dispute: the faculty of self-perception" (114). At this point in time, it is important to discuss the development of preferences amongst men. According to Rousseau, "People grow accustomed to consider different objects and to make comparisons; imperceptibly they acquire ideas of merit and beauty which produce sentiments of preference" (148).

From this statement, one could conclude that preferences arose from the comparison of objects and which of those objects held more merit or pleasure to the individual, who, because he was self-aware, knew what affected him most beneficially. Comparison, then, would be a form of or developed from reasoning between the qualities of two objects. If man then has preference between two objects, especially in the case of members of the opposite gender, he must desire that which he prefers the most. If there is not reciprocity in this engagement, or man is incapable of satiating this new desire, then man's desire goes unfulfilled, and this type of *dependent* desire, in itself, is the first manifestation of misery in humanity. Dependent desires, only arising from man's preferences, created wants that were out of the individual's capacity to satisfy. Previously, before the progression of faculties, there were only independent desires. According to Rousseau, "...[early man's] desires [did] not exceed his physical needs," to which his physical capacities adapted to fulfill (116, 105). Therefore, by Rousseau's definition of misery, these dependent desires manifested the first misery within humanity.

Being conscious of himself and his tendencies, man, with reflection and the ability to reason, "...[saw] that [other man] all behaved as he would have done under similar circumstances, he concluded that their way of thinking and feeling conformed entirely to his own" (144). This, when in combination of preferences, made man conscious that his brethren also had preferences. Upon this discovery, "[man] began to look at the others and to want to be looked at himself, and public esteem had a value," and man realized that those with superior traits became more considered, and consequently wanted himself to be most considered (149). According to Rousseau, "from these first preferences were born...vanity and contempt" (149). Vanity, as the dependent desire of being most highly considered by others, is the second manifestation of misery in the human condition.

Once vanity had been established within humanity, it soon combined with other secondary faculties to lead to additional misery, especially in the case of foresight. Foresight allowed man to, "...envisage so far in advance the advantages they could gain..." (152). After the discovery of agriculture, man would have been able to reason that he with the most crops would be highly considered, and he with the most land could grow the most crops. Consequently, out of vanity, he would have labored over his crops and would have staked off property to claim as his own on the basis that his labor entitled him to that land (154). Simultaneously, man would have, "...observed that it was useful for a single person to have provisions for two..." (151). When man joined these two thoughts, he would have realized the benefit to having other men work for him on his property, and thus a new dependent desire would have been formed. Also, a sense of power and, thus, inequality would have been created: those with property and those without, or, in a sense, the rich and the poor (154-155). Eventually, according to Rousseau, the rich would have become dependent upon the poor to produce their goods and the poor dependent on the rich for help (156). In this relationship alone, no new type of misery is added, only additional misery within dependent desires. However, when combined with man's ability to resist the rules of nature, and thus the ability to deny natural pity, man would then have desire to make his brethren suffer, so long as it was for his own benefit. Rousseau stated, "...as men began to look to the future and as they all saw themselves with some goods to lose, there was not one of them who did not have to fear reprisals against themselves for wrongs he might do to another," as well as, "...the fervor to raise one's relative fortune less out of true need than in order to place oneself above others, inspires in all men a base inclination to harm each other" (154, 156). With inequality and the desire to harm others for one's own benefit, man created slavery and other such institutions. It is highly plausible that those excesses and deficiencies mentioned in Rousseau's definition of 'suffering of the soul' were formed out of this system, as those with power would have access and preference toward them, and thus the third and final type of misery was instilled in humanity.

If one accepts Rousseau's premise for what constitutes as the three distinctive human capacities endowed upon humanity by nature, it is easy to see how these qualities would have evolved in such a way into placing all of humanity in the general condition of misery. From whatever start humanity had, it was doomed by nature itself to be miserable. Nature, from the beginning, prepared man to become miserable by equipping him with those certain faculties, and time sealed this reality to be a forevermore permanent condition. Therefore, man cannot escape his misery insofar as he cannot escape his humanity.

Rousseau has all but proven that man cannot go back to his savage state. Therefore, this is not a viable solution to end his misery. However, he did provide insights as to how to possibly, not necessarily eliminate this misery, but minimize it. According to the misery caused by dependent desires, the misery derives from the desire not being fulfilled, which, because the desires can be inessential to survival, the misery comes from the *expectation* of the desire being fulfilled. Therefore, to combat this misery, man would have to understand that those desires are artificial and also dependent, and consequently realize that it is unrealistic for them to be satiated. This would account for why Rousseau presented his *Second Discourse* in the manner that he did, if his goal was to enlighten the reader to those dependent desires. Because man cannot revert back to his early state, the only way to then overcome this obstacle would be to further increase man's perfectibility, or at least his enlightenment, so that he would realize the irrationality of the expectation to have dependent desires fulfilled. If such a feat was accomplished, the strength of vanity within man would decrease, and consequently more misery would be abated.

Rousseau claimed that man's golden age was when his first and, at the time, only dependent desire of love was reciprocated and fulfilled (150-151). Because Rousseau provided examples of excesses that caused misery, there would have to be a mean, to which misery would be minimized. This mean could be the abolition of expectations of fulfillment for dependent desires, save the desire for reciprocated love. Thus, the best life, or at least the life with the least misery, would require the enhancement of reason and the fulfillment of the original dependent desire for the reciprocity of love. However, a problem arises.

If man's enlightenment increases, then, by the logic presented previously, the capacity of comparison would also increase, thus causing further preferences. The problem then arises that man would have such distinguished preferences, that his choosing a partner to obtain the reciprocation of love would become more daunting and challenging, and obtaining the reciprocity of love from that specific person would also become a greater challenge, which therefore increases misery, as the longing for the original dependent desire would go unfulfilled. So unless the capacities of reason exceeded those of comparison, man, at the cost of some of his misery, would increase his misery in other manners. Ultimately, man would have to realize that his preferences were counterproductive to his happiness, and thus would need to overcome those preferences and settle with the first partner that would reciprocate his love, as this would be the rational decision to minimize his misery. Again, the question that needs to be asked becomes if man's capacity to compare increases, and thus his preferences, relative to the increase to the capacity of reason, can man truly eliminate all of his secondary dependent desires and fulfill his original? Because perfectibility is not unlimited, and thus man's ability to reason cannot be perfected, it seems logical to assume that man would never be capable of 'out-reasoning' all of his preferences. Thus he would never be able to eliminate all of his secondary dependent desires, while easily fulfilling his original. However, the problems do not end here.

If man increases his ability to reason, it is a possibility that this increase would be complimented by an increase in vanity, as man would see that he is exceeding his fellow man in an admirable trait, thus making himself 'better' than his brethren. Thus, an increase in reasoning could potentially deepen the misery caused from vanity, unless man increased his reasoning solely for the sake of itself out the independent desire to minimize his own misery. In addition, it is possible that out of this vanity, man would have further difficulty in satiating his original dependent desires for other reasons than those mentioned prior, as he would then have a greater difficulty finding someone he deemed worthy of his love. Again, this would be a bidirectional problem, as both individuals would have to deem each other worthy. If man was able to able to increase his reasoning to the point where he was able to overcome his preferences, and thus settle with the first partner who reciprocated his love, this still opens up room for his vanity to increase, as he would now be superior to his brethren in that regard.

Ultimately, if and only if man could increase his reasoning to the point of overcoming his preferences and did so solely for the sake of itself to eliminate his own misery, provided that this can be done *without* needing perfectibility to be unlimited, can man escape misery. However, it seems logically necessary for man to be completely enlightened to do so, and thus it seems there is no possible way out of this condition. Therefore, with this being stated, it would appear that the best course for man to take in life would be the *pursuit* of alleviating self-misery. Ultimately, man would have to *attempt* to increase his reasoning so that he could understand his expectations of secondary dependent desires being fulfilled are irrational, be conscious of and eliminate his vanity, and overcome his preferences (though this still requires a second party to do the same). However, if the pursuit to alleviate self-misery is what is best, it would only minimize misery, as for this pursuit to exist, one must be experiencing misery. So once more it must be stated that man cannot escape his misery insofar as he cannot escape his humanity, but, with the proper development of faculties, man can at least minimize it.

Rashness in Battle:
A Study of *Temeritas* in Book Twenty-Two of Livy's *Ab Urbe Condita*

Tim Knoepke

Temeritas, defined by Cassell's New Latin Dictionary as 'chance,' 'rashness,' and 'heedlessness,' has many different usages throughout the twenty-second book of Livy's *Ab Urbe Condita.*[1] It plays a substantial role and is used eighteen times throughout the book, including its noun, adverbial, and adjectival forms. It is coupled with many varying words and a part of important phrases. I am studying *temeritas,* along with its relationship with *fortuna,* because I want to find out what role it had to play in the 22nd book of Livy and why that role was so large in comparison to the previous book in order to understand how a *temeraria* nature brought about such catastrophic defeats for the Romans. As the dominant influence in a man's mind once it has been given free control, *temeritas* enslaves its host to the enemy and makes him a tool to bring about his own destruction. *Fortuna* also, by means of short-lived success, nourishes *temeritas* and is relied upon most because to act with rashness is to leave the result of battle to the fickle force of the unknown which *fortuna* is. Yet, caution, careful planning, reason, and prudence stand as the opponents of *temeritas* which the wise commander, such as Fabius, relies upon

---

[1] Simpson, D P. *Cassell's New Latin Dictionary: Latin-English, English-Latin.* New York: Funk & Wagnalls, 1960.

to bring him true and long-lasting success. Ultimately, *temeritas* serves as the prime *exemplum* from Livy in book twenty-two on how not to conduct oneself in war.

The Commanders of *Temeritas*

First, a few words need to be said about the commanders involved. In book twenty-two, Livy attributes certain Roman men with temeritas as well as showing how the enemy Hannibal used that temeritas to his advantage. These men are Gaius Flaminius, Hannibal Barca, Marcus Minucius, Quintus Fabius Maximus, and Gaius Terentius Varro. A short biography of each man will be included in the section of the paper where they are first mentioned and where it is necessary to understand his character.

Hannibal Barca was the commander of the Carthaginian army during the Second Punic War, which is sometimes referred to as the Hannibalic War due to the monumental role he played. A long description of his character is provided in 21.4., but a few of his greatest strengths which should be pointed out are his "reckless courage" united with the "greatest judgment," his ability to "inspire his men with...confidence and daring," and his lack of desire for any kind of physical pleasure.[2] He is still regarded as one of the greatest military commanders of all time. His main role in this paper is as the supreme commander of events, manipulating

---

[2] Benjamin O. Foster, Alfred C. Schlesinger, and Russel M. Geer. *Livy: With an English Translation.* Cambridge, Mass: Harvard University Press, 1967. P.11.

his enemies to serve his will and using their weaknesses to his advantage.

Gaius Flaminius became famous for his defeat and subsequent death at the hands of the Carthaginians during the Battle of Lake Trasimene in 217 B.C. E., after falling headlong into a trap laid by Hannibal.[3] He is seen as a prime example of the negative result of *temeritas* in decision making as he rushed into a trap without first reconnoitering the land ahead and not learning anything about his enemy. Flaminius' character is otherwise less developed in the history due to his untimely death as well as his only action being in a single battle.

Marcus Minucius was named to the office of master of horse under the dictatorship of Fabius Maximus.[4] He proved himself to be a very headstrong man, with a fierce craving for glory. He felt that it was through swift action and daring that the Romans would achieve victory over Hannibal.[5] This placed him as the greatest advocate of *temeritas*. He was defeated by Hannibal in a battle which could have had as great of a slaughter as Cannae, if not for the aid of Fabius.[6] Fabius rescued the army from utter destruction and afterwards Minucius pledged himself to the command of Fabius. His speech to his troops serves to show how deep of an effect the defeat had on sobering him up, finally

[3] Foster. P. 209. Livy 22.3.
[4] Foster. P. 227. Livy 22.8
[5] Foster. P. 241-243. Livy 22.12.
[6] Foster. P. 295-301. Livy 22.28-29.

opening his eyes to his own *temeritas*.[7] His story, overall, is an example of how far reaching the extent of *temeritas'* power is and how powerful, in contrast, a force is needed to check *temeritas*.

Quintus Fabius Maximus appears as if out of thin air in Livy's history, which could be due in part to the loss of the books immediately preceding book twenty-one.[8] He was named to the dictatorship following the catastrophe at Lake Trasimene in 217 B.C. and the death of Flaminius. He was the greatest threat to Hannibal's conquest during the beginning of the war, countering his rapid movement with delaying tactics.[9] This method of waging war proved to be unpopular amongst the general populace and led to many arguments as well as the questioning of his leadership from his colleagues. He is the quintessential example of how to oppose *temeritas* as he strove throughout book twenty-two to defeat Hannibal through careful planning and not rushing into battle. He, therefore, rightfully earned the title "Cunctator" (Delayer).

Gaius Terentius Varro rose to the office of consul through trickery and endearing himself to the people.[10] By constantly undermining the actions of Fabius, Varro made himself popular amongst the plebians and used this popularity to win their vote.[11] He had no experience of battle and is marked as being worse than

---

[7] The full speech of Minucius can be found in Livy 22.29.
[8] Foster. P. 227. Livy 22.8.
[9] Foster. P. 251, 277-279, 295 Livy 22.15., 22.23., 22.28.
[10] Foster. P. 289. Livy 22.26.1-2.
[11] Foster. P. 289. Livy 22.26.3-4.

Flaminius in the sense that he proved himself to be mad before he even entered into his office. During his consulship, he led the Roman army into the battle of Cannae in 216 B.C. and caused the subsequent destruction through his poor leadership. He escaped the battle with his life and left his fellow consul Aemilius Paulus to die. He was the sole cause of what would arguably be designated the worst defeat in Roman history, as well as the greatest example of the monumental destruction which temeritas is able to bring about.

The Nature of *Temeritas*

Temeritas is first of all to be understood as an excessive reliance on *fortuna*, which came to be construed as recklessness. *Fortuna* is the unknown and mysterious entity which governs events and is forever unpredictable.[12] To understand the role of *temeritas*, one must first understand its nature and understand how one comes to be reckless. The very first usage of *temeritas* in book twenty-two offers some insight into its nature. "This native rashness had been nourished by the success which fortune had bestowed on him in political and military enterprises."[13] This passage presents the idea that *temeritas* is an innate quality. *Insitus* is a word which means 'implanted' and 'innate,' but is translated by Foster as

---

[12] Davies, Jason P. *Rome's Religious History: Livy, Tacitus, and Ammianus on Their Gods.* Cambridge, UK: Cambridge University Press, 2004. Print. "Fortuna is construed as a more willful entity "governing" events in a more general way... fortuna is an agent in a more nebulous and circumscribed manner." P.117

[13] Foster. P. 209. Livy 22.3.4. hanc insitam ingenio eius temeritatem fortuna prospero civilibus bellicisque rebus successu aluerat

"native." This rashness had been 'implanted' into the *ingenium*, 'nature' or 'character,' of Flaminius. The small, but vital, difference between an 'implanted' and 'innate' temeritas makes it difficult to say for certain whether *temeritas* is a part of a man's character from birth or if it is built up over a long period of time. This means that *temeritas* has had a sort of leeching effect: any good qualities the general may have originally possessed in his nature have been destroyed and replaced by *temeritas*. *Temeritas* becomes a part of a man's personal character and, therefore, influences every decision he makes.

Another aspect of the nature of *temeritas* is its inability to be controlled. "All this caused Hannibal a twofold joy, for...he reckoned on entrapping the uncontrolled rashness of Minucius after his own fashion."[14] *Temeritas* is described by the adjective *liber* in this situation. According to *Cassell's*, *liber* is an adjective meaning 'unrestrained,' 'unencumbered,' and 'uninhibited.' This simple adjective shows just how much of a danger *temeritas* poses. A *temeritas* that is *libera* means that not only will the man it is attributed to act rashly, despite his better nature, he will not pay attention to the advice of those counseling him. When translated as 'inhibited,' it is rather easy to connect *libera temeritas* to the effects of alcohol on a man's ability to make wise decisions. Polybius himself, a famous Greek historian who first wrote a history of the Punic Wars and greatly influenced Livy's history,

---

[14] Foster. P. 295. Livy 22.28.2. Duplex inde Hannibali gaudium fuit... nam et liberam Minuci temeritatem se suo modo captuturum

remarks in his history that alcoholism as a seriously harmful vice for a general to have. "...While there are many others so fond of wine that they cannot go to sleep without fuddling themselves with drink; and some, owing to their abandonment to venery and the consequent derangement of their minds, have not only ruined their countries and their fortunes but brought their lives to a shameful end."[15] Therefore, *temeritas* makes a man no better at making wise decisions than a drunkard and shows how much of a threat *temeritas* poses as a result of this.

Fortuna and Temeritas

Yet how does *temeritas* grow in a man's mind to the point where it becomes uncontrollable and makes him unable to think through a situation? The answer is *fortuna*. Of all the words with which *temeritas* is paired or associated, there is none more important than that of *fortuna*. "As a deity, she was mother, nurse, provider, guardian, friend, and enemy, to the Roman, and the child of Jupiter himself."[16] *Fortuna* served to embody the mysterious force in warfare, the incalculable element which no commander could control completely. Originally, *temeritas* was viewed as an unhealthy or dangerous reliance on *fortuna*, according to the Oxford Latin Dictionary.[17] To the Romans,

[15] Polybius 3.81.5-6. Paton, W. R., Polybius. *The Histories*. Cambridge: Harvard University Press, 1954.

[16] Patch, Howard R. *The Tradition of the Goddess Fortuna in Roman Literature and the Transitional Period*. Northampton, Mass: Smith College, 1922. P.133.

[17] Glare, P G. W. *Oxford Latin Dictionary*. Oxford Clarendon Press, 1982.

fortuna was a fickle friend, not to be relied upon more than was necessary, so it seems only natural the use of *temeritas* developed from 'a reliance on *fortuna*' to 'rashness.'[18]

Revisiting the opening quote from Livy, "this native rashness had been nourished by the success which Fortune had bestowed on him in political and military enterprises," *fortuna* plays a role in the development of *temeritas* in one's mind. Fortune does not create rashness.[19] That fault lies with the man alone. It serves only to nourish and cause *temeritas* to grow, acting almost as a nourishing mother if one may see it that way. *Fortuna* brings about this growth through success. "*Fortuna* is not, however, always favourable... inherent in *fortuna's* gifts is the dispensation of failure or loss after a run of success."[20] Success gives one a false sense of courage which allows him to believe that his success will continue only by the sheer coincidence that he got lucky in the past.[21] Success becomes, therefore, merely a tool of *fortuna* used on rash men so as to eventually bring about their downfall.[22]

The extent to which one relies on *fortuna*, and therefore how rash he proves to be, determines how controlling of an effect *fortuna* will have. "This proposal by no means suited Quintus

---

[18] Patch. P.142.
[19] Foster. P.209. Livy 22.3.4. hanc insitam ingenio eius temeritatem fortuna prospero civilibus bellicisque rebus successu aluerat.
[20] Davies. P.119.
[21] Kajanto, Iiro. *God and Fate in Livy*. Turku: Turun Yliopiston Kustantama, 1957. "If fortuna-tyche shows someone favour, she does so only to turn success into misfortune before long; otherwise she heaps successes on people who do not deserve them." P.76.
[22] Kajanto. "Livy has two different views on the way in which fortuna's favour turns out to be dangerous. In some cases fortuna annihilates a man by letting him enjoy too much success and so blinding his judgment." P.83.

Fabius for he saw that everything which his rash colleague should have got control of would be controlled by Fortune."[23] This passage lends some evidence to the previous claim that *temeritas* is uncontrolled and free; it also shows what force takes control once a man has given up his own control due to his *temeritas: fortuna.* *Fortuna* here is the unknown or mysterious force, so really what Minucius is doing in this passage is taking no control at all.[24] He would rather rely on the unknown and hope that chance will win his battles, that to have to put forth his own effort and willpower. *Temeritas* then becomes a true form of weakness and, contrary to the idea of rashness as vigorous action, mental laziness.

"There it is," said Fabius, when first the cries of the frightened soldiers were heard, and then the confusion in the distant battle-line became discernible; "misfortune has not overtaken rashness more quickly than I feared."[25] Through its nourishment of *temeritas, fortuna* has finally given a general, in this case Minucius, the confidence to offer battle. But because Minucius chose to offer battle without first laying plans or learning about the nature of his enemy, he has set himself up for destruction. A slightly different translation of this passage offers a clearer view of the role of *fortuna:* "Fortune has not latched on to

---

[23] Foster. P.293. Livy. 22.27.8. Q. Fabio haudquaquam id placere: omnia enim fortunam eam habituram quaecumque temeritas collegae habuisset.

[24] Walsh, P G. *Livy: His Historical Aims and Methods.* Cambridge University Press, 1961. "In the primitive Roman theology, where each individual deity had his or her peculiar province, Fortuna supervised the incalculable element of life." P.56.

[25] Foster. P.297-299. Livy 22.29.1. tum Fabius primo clamore paventium audito dein conspecta procul turbata acie, "Ita est" inquit; "non celeres quam timui deprendit fortuna temeritatem."

rashness more quickly than I feared."[26] The Latin verb *deprendere* used here means 'to snatch' or 'to seize."[27] This seems to imply that fortune has the ability to sense weakness, in this case *temeritas*, and punishes it. Minucius' rashness, which success and fortune had previously nourished, now is used against him by fortune to coax him into offering battle. He rushed into battle and faced a general far superior to him.[28] The rashness of Minucius ultimately resulted in defeat at the hands of Hannibal.[29] Rashness naturally leads to misfortune. Fabius states that he had foreseen this and warned the Senate, as well as the people, and still nothing is done. This means that rashness may not always lead to destruction, if it is curbed beforehand. But if left unattended, a result such as this is what is to be expected. Overall, *temeritas* is punished by *fortuna*; it is able to be foreseen, but because *temeritas* is *liber*, as discussed earlier. It refuses to head any counsel which seeks to curb it.

Fortuna has previously been described as taking the role of the nourishing mother, but another role which *fortuna* has in conjunction with *temeritas* is that of the "bestower."[30] Patch explains it thus:

> The fundamental idea of "Fortuna" is the bestower; the connotation is that of the creative goddess...A man's attitude toward the bestowing force depends

---

[26] My own personal translation, in an effort to better explain and understand this passage.
[27] OLD
[28] See Livy 21.4. for a complete account of Hannibal's character.
[29] See Livy 22.28-30. for a complete account of Minucius' defeat by Hannibal.
[30] Patch. P.133.

on the kind of life he is living. The life that causes a strong belief in the element of chance may be of two kinds:--A man may feel himself too weak to cope with the external powers, and may consequently believe that he is in the control of an outer destiny. On the other hand, he may be so physically vigorous that he launches forth boldly in the unknown, and then the vast unconquerable spaces of that region impress themselves up on him. Under these circumstances, again, he feels himself at the mercy of the outer forces. He is less inclined to trust his own wits, or to believe in free-will; he is more likely to speak of chance.[31]

Throughout his history, Livy presents *fortuna* as a bestowing force, supplying various men and generals with a situation to either excel or fail. *Fortuna* does not sway the outcome of events one way or the other; it is up to the men involved, in accordance with their nature, to decide what the outcome will be.[32] "But even Fortune furnished material to the recklessness and over-hasty temper of the consul."[33] With *temeritas, fortuna* is supplying situations, seen here as a proverbial fanning of the flames, in which a man will have the opportunity to act rash. It is the consul Varro himself, in this case, who is bringing about his own downfall, not *fortuna* forcing him to act in a certain way or turning the tide against him. According to

---

[32] Levene, D S. *Religion in Livy.* Leiden: E.J. Brill, 1993. "More likely is that Livy is playing down the role of the supernatural in the battle in order to emphasize the part played by the military genius of Hannibal, a genius which he is magnifying in the order to magnify the ultimate Roman victory. More generally, however, this is the first example of a phenomenon which we shall often have occasion to notice: that, although Livy often shows the supernatural at work in his narrative, when it comes to the central battles of his history, he prefers to play it down, and to attribute defeat and victory to human factors alone." P.49.

the categories of Patch outlined in the previous quotation, Varro shows himself to be the second kind of man, a man of weak mind and weaker self-confidence, allowing himself to be effected substantially by *fortuna* due to his *temeritas*. *Temeritas* then is the negative force, found in the minds of weak men, which drives a man to destruction after *fortuna* has bestowed a situation upon him.

The Effects of Rashness on the Enemy

Hannibal, being the military genius that his is, finds ways throughout book twenty two to use *temeritas* to his advantage and it ultimately is the cause of success for him in many battles. *Temeritas* becomes a tool in his hands.

> All this caused Hannibal a twofold joy, for, fully acquainted as he was with whatever went on amongst his enemies both from much information brought in by deserters and from the discoveries of his own spies, he reckoned on entrapping the uncontrolled rashness of Minucius after his own fashion, while he saw that the sagacity of Fabius had been deprived of half its strength.[34]

Livy presents Hannibal as being the complete opposite of rash. Because Hannibal is "fully acquainted" with the terrain and the enemy commanders he must face, he is able to use *temeritas*

---

[33] Foster. P.337. Livy 22.41.1. ceterum temeritati consulis ac praepropero ingenio materiam etiam fortuna dedit.

[34] Foster. P.295. Livy 22.28.1. Duplex inde Hannibali gaudium fuit—neque enim quicquam eorum quae apud hostes agerentur eum fallebat, et perfugis multa indicantibus et per suos explorantem;—nam et liberam Minuci temeritatem se suo modo captuturum et sollertiae Fabi dimidium virium decessisse.

against Minucius. This *temeritas*, described once again as *liber*, freely leaves control of the situation to an outside force, in this case Hannibal. He had total control while Minucius was free. Hannibal's success as a commander, especially in his encounters with Minucius, then can be attributed to his ability to entrap the mind of his enemies. *Temeritas* served as his greatest tool in the early battles of the 2nd Punic War as he manipulated this trait to obey his will. *Temeritas* then becomes the master of a man's nature and enslaved, rather than freed, him. The power lies with the force that held the chains.

Temeritas not only enslaves the man guilty of it, but causes widespread harm. In the previous passage, *temeritas* also negatively affected the cleverness of Fabius; *temeritas* opposed *sollertia*, translated by Foster above in English as 'sagacity,' and deprived it of its power. To the well-organized and prepared mind of Hannibal, *temeritas* is seen as a tool to cripple the power of cleverness in his enemy Fabius. It becomes all the more dangerous as it is given more and more power. Fabius, the only one capable of countering Minucius' malignant nature, is robbed of his most precious asset. He may attempt to save the Romans from complete destruction, but he will have little effect with his diminished power. *Temeritas* has shackled him as well and given him a short leash with which to act in opposition.

Temeritas, as free and harmful as it was, brings about only contempt and disgust from good commanders. It is seen easily by enemies while that man remains oblivious. "He who dares all things will earn Hannibal's contempt; he who does nothing rashly will inspire him with fear."[35] *Temeritas* brings about contempt from Hannibal. A true general makes no move without planning it out accordingly. *Audentem,* translated as "who dares all things" and related to *audacia,* the word for 'boldness' and 'daring.' even presents itself as a negative quality.[36] A wise man, much less a general, knows better than to believe he will have success in everything he does. He does only what he knows he will succeed at, bringing up the point once again that nothing should be left to *fortuna. Temeritas* clouds, even to the point of blinding, the mind to the situation, and the resulting harm in which a rash man places himself.

The blinding power of *temeritas* leaves the power of an opponent ineffective to curb that destructive nature. When that opponent is a friend or colleague, that effectiveness becomes complete. "The dictator had found his master of the horse intolerable: what power or influence would a consul have over a turbulent and headstrong colleague?"[37] *Temeritas* and *seditiosus* are paired together as adjectives attributed to Minucius. *Seditiosus* is a result of someone's rash inner nature. In his haste to fight, Minucius alienates himself from his colleague by quarreling with him and only makes the situation worse. Try as he might to curb

---

[35] Foster. P.333. Livy. 22.39.20. omnia audentem contemnet Hannibal, nihil temere agentem metuet.
[36] OLD
[37] Foster. P.335. Livy. 22.40.2. dictatori magistrum equitum intolerabilem fuisse: quid consuli adversus collegam seditiosum ac temerarium virium atque auctoritatis fore?

temeritas, Fabius is ignored and is left with no more power than a bystander. Therefore, rashness becomes uncontrollable, not just when someone allows it to be. No one else can change the course once a rash man has his eyes blinded to the inevitable result of destruction which *temeritas* will cause.

The gods and other outside forces are not the major players in events, but allow men and their own qualities to decide the outcome. A theory for why Livy placed *temeritas* as the cause of all the Roman defeats in book twenty-two of his history is put forward by Levene.

> More likely is that Livy is playing down the role of the supernatural in the battle [of Cannae] in order to emphasize the part played by the military genius of Hannibal, a genius which he is magnifying in the order to magnify the ultimate Roman victory. More generally, however, this is the first example of a phenomenon which we shall often have occasion to notice: that, although Livy often shows the supernatural at work in his narrative, when it comes to the central battles of his history, he prefers to play it down, and to attribute defeat and victory to human factors alone.[38]

Levene believes that Livy emphasized the power of character traits such as *temeritas* in the early battles of the war to show how much the Romans had to learn so as to achieve the final victory. *Temeritas*, a "human factor," is the sole cause of destruction.[39] Fortune and religious observance, the focal points of study for Levene in this book, become minor entities, especially in book

---

[38] Levene. P.49.

twenty-two, nurturing "human factors" so that the outside powers are less powerful. Livy wants his readers to see *temeritas* as an example of how not to conduct a war or act when in a position of power.

In a return again to the power of success on a rash mind, Hannibal uses *temeritas,* nourished by success in battle, as a tool to bring about victory for himself. The new consul, Varro, had been judged by Fabius as even more rash and dangerous than his predecessor Minucius. And this Hannibal will use to his advantage. "Hannibal was not greatly disconcerted by his reverse; indeed he rejoiced that the hook should have been baited, as it were, for the rashness of the more impetuous consul."[40] The much more experienced and more intelligent general Hannibal understood that one defeat, or victory, did not decide how the rest of events would play out. This had been proven in his previous encounters with Minucius, where good fortune, synonymous with success, had influenced Minucius to make rash decisions.[41] Hannibal rather used his defeat as a tool. It inflated Varro's rashness even, as fortune frequently did. The verb here in the phrase "baiting the hook" is *inesco,* which means 'entice.'[42] Therefore, Hannibal

---

[39] Levene. P.49.

[40] Foster. P.337. Livy. 22.41.4. Hannibal id damnum haud aegerrime pati; quin potius gaudere velut inescatam temeritatem ferocioris consulis ac novorum maxime militum esse.

[41] Foster. P.293. Livy. 22.27.4-5. ergo secuturum se fortunam suam, si dictator in cunctatione ac segnitie deorum hominumque iudicio damnata perstaret...he would therefore follow up his good fortune, if the dictator persisted in that dilatory and inactive course which gods and men had united in condemning...

[42] OLD

enticed *temeritas* with an artificial success and showed how it could become a dangerous and powerful tool in the hands of an enemy.

Opposition to *Temeritas*

Of all the generals which commanded the Roman army during the Second Punic War, there was none who presented himself as more of an opponent to *temeritas* than Quintus Fabius Maximus, later given the title of the Cunctator. He understood the danger which *temeritas* posed to the Roman army and recognized the brilliance which Hannibal displayed in using *temeritas* against his opposing commanders. Throughout book twenty-two, Livy, through the many speeches and commentaries on warfare from Fabius Maximus, highlighted the qualities which most contradicted rashness and a reliance on an outside force, such as *fortuna*. In this way, Livy succeeded in teaching his readers how to combat *temeritas* and chronicled the effort of the Romans on their path to reverse their defeats.

After his previous relatively easy success against the rashness of the general Flaminius, Hannibal was wary of the new elected consul and threat he posed. "This policy, though it occasioned Hannibal no small anxiety—for he saw that the Romans had finally chosen a military leader who waged war as reason and not as blind chance dictated."[43] Even from his first impression,

---

[43] Foster. P.277, 279. Livy. 22.23.2-3 Quae ut Hannibalem non mediocri sollictum cura habebat. Tandem eum militiae magistrum delegisse Romanos cernentem, qui bellum ratione non fortuna gereret.

Fabius was a strong opponent of rashness and leaving any outcome to chance. Fabius championed rational thought and methodical plan of action, embodied in the Latin word *ratio*. Hidden behind the surface conflict of war fought sword to sword, there was a battle of rational thought and military strategy against *temeritas* and its nourishing mother *fortuna*. Yet this battle was not strictly fought between the Carthaginians and Romans. It was fought among each commander and soldier, even those on the same side. Hannibal, with clear eyes not clouded by *temeritas*, knew Fabius would rely as lightly on the unknown as he possibly could and make every decision only after careful thought. *Temeritas* would not be the tool he would be able to rely on to achieve victory.

Some of the qualities which Fabius first presented as the most danger to *temeritas* were caution and careful planning. "He (Fabius) hoped that what was done with care and caution would turn out for the best: rashness was not only foolish but had hitherto been unfortunate as well. It was quite apparently his own intention to choose a safe course rather than a hasty one."[44] Fabius, in the fashion of Hannibal, looks down upon the rash and knows what the result of such action will be. *Temeritas* is described, therefore, as *stulta* and *infelix*. One must rather act *caute* and *consulte*. In the lines which follow, *tuta* is contrasted against *celer consilium*. To act with any kind of speed in planning is to act

---

[44] Foster. P.327. Livy. 22.38.11-12. Optare ut quae caute ac consulte gesta essent satis prospere eventirent; temeritatem, praeterquam quod stulta sit, infelicem etiam ad id locorum fuisse. Sua sponte apparebat tuta celeribus consiliis praepositurum.

rashly and not only is foolish, but unsafe. A general must have the situation carefully planned out and not rush forward if he desires to see any kind of favorable or safe result.

No matter how effective this kind of action may be, it will not always meet with positive criticism or support unless it reaps immediate successful results.

> The dictator refrained from making speeches to the people, in a cause that was far from popular. Even the senate listened coldly when he spoke in high terms of the enemy, and charging the reverses of the past two years to the rashness and ignorance of the Roman generals, declared that the master of horse must answer to him for having fought against his orders.[45]

The Romans had suffered defeat after defeat in the opening battles of the Second Punic War, yet they still had not learned, or even understood, the reason for these defeats. Fabius Maximus, though, knew and had put into place a strategy which would ultimately prove successful if upheld. He recognized *temeritas* and *inscitia* as the bringers of destruction. Notice that Fabius praises Hannibal while condemning the Romans. He wants the Carthaginian to serve as a good example to generals which the Romans must learn from to correct their mistakes. The immediate success which *temeritas* at times yields appeased the masses because they were did not recognize the brilliance of the delaying strategy and

---

[45] Foster. P.287. Livy. 22.25.12. dictator contionibus se abstinuit in actione minime populari. Ne in senatu quidem satis aequis auribus audiebatur, cum hostem verbis extolleret biennique clades per temeritatem atque inscitiam ducum acceptas referret et magistro equitum quod contra dictum suum pugnasset rationem diceret reddendam esse.

therefore reacted negatively to it. This is summed up later on in the book in these words of Fabius: "I had rather a wise enemy should fear you than foolish citizens should praise you."[46] Fabius had the answer and still he was not respected by the people.

The quality which most combats *temeritas* and leads one down a path of success is that of *consilium*. Defined as 'prudence,' 'deliberation,' or 'counsel,' *consilium* is remarked upon numerous times by Livy, through Fabius Maximus, as the only proper plan of action to take against the tactics of Hannibal.[47] "He would therefore never voluntarily relinquish that share that he possessed of the power to guide the campaign prudently."[48] *Consilium* is here translated as "prudently" by Foster and "proper direction" by Selincourt.[49] Another reference to *consilium* puts it this way: "The dictator encamped in the country about Larinum, and being summoned thence to Rome on religious business, commanded, counseled, and all but entreated the master of the horse to put more trust in prudence than in fortune, and rather to imitate his strategy than that of Sempronius and Flaminius."[50] Selincourt translates much closer to the Latin than Foster does.[51] Where

---

[46] Foster. P.333. Livy. 22.39.20. malo te sapiens hostis metuat quam stulti cives laudent.
[47] OLD
[48] Foster. P.293. Livy. 22.27.9. itaque se nunquam volentem parte qua posset rerum consilio gerendarum cessurum.
[49] Selincourt A. De, and Betty Radice. *The War with Hannibal: Books Xxi-Xxx of the History of Rome from Its Foundation.* Baltimore: Penguin Books, 1965. P.126.
[50] Foster. P.261. Livy. 22.18.8. dictator in Larinati agro castra communiit. Inde sacrorum causa Romam revocatus, non imperio modo, sed consilio etiam ac prope precibus agens cum magistro equitum ut plus consilio quam fortunae confidant et se potius ducem quam Sempronium Flaminiumque imitetur.
[51] Selincourt. "After these moves Fabius was recalled to Rome to attend to certain religious matters; before he left he spoke with his master of horse: what he was not only a

Selincourt chooses to translate the phrases entirely as "what he was not only a command, it was the most earnest advice: nay, he almost begged him with prayers," Foster condenses these phrases into the verbs "commanded, counseled, and all but entreated."[52] Both translators still retain the general idea of each Latin phrase, though one should rely on *consilium* rather than *fortuna* if he desires to be successful. Fabius feels it is his duty as a general, much less a man, to not let his men be led into destruction. Fortune continues to be seen by Fabius as a fickle friend and he wishes Minucius to rely on his strategy than fortune. Therefore, to plan out one's attack well is to act prudently/wisely and *consilium* is then marked as the foremost opponent to *temeritas*.

Conclusion

Book twenty-two serves as an *exemplum* for what a rash reliance on *fortuna* will result in. This is a vital component of Livy' history and explains why *fortuna* and *temeritas* become part of the vocabulary in the *Ab Urbe Condita*. Jane Chaplin thoroughly explored this topic in her book "Livy's Exemplary History" and best explains *exempla* in this way:

> Exempla are a rhetorical device, and their malleability springs in part from the fact that as such, they have to fit multiple arguments or even both sides of a single argument. Livy's use of exempla confirms the rhetorical skill for which he was praised. But it is also central to his view of

---

command, it was the most earnest advice: nay, he almost begged him with prayers to act prudently instead of trusting to luck, and to imitate himself, Fabius, in his strategy rather than Sempronius or Flaminius." P.126

[52] Selincourt. P.114. Foster. P.261.

history. The ability to manipulate an audience's perception of the past may come from oratory, but Livy converts it into a tool of historical interpretation. Thus the persuasive representations of Cannae, Caudium, and historical exempla generally help Livy to control how his contemporaries outside the text can learn from the lessons offered to the audiences inside it.[53]

Therefore, *temeritas*, both in the history and in the minds of its readers, offers a lesson to be studied and interpreted as each reader sees fit. The lesson here is that *temeritas* is always a negative quality, nourished by *fortuna* through success, and leads one down the path to destruction. By means of *consilium, ratio, cautio,* and *consultis*, one is able to oppose *temeritas*. Fabius serves as the foremost example of how to do this and caused Hannibal to fear him as a dangerous enemy. The inclusion of *temeritas* and *fortuna* in the book twenty-two therefore becomes a personal message from Livy to his readers as an *exemplum* of how to act in warfare. Book twenty-two, overall, was to serve as an example of how not to conduct warfare while using Fabius to present the qualities which would later bring success once the Romans had their eyes finally opened to the dangers of *temeritas* after the colossal slaughter at Cannae.

---

[53] Chaplin, Jane D. *Livy's Exemplary History.* Oxford University Press, 2000. Print. P.72.

Bibliography

Primary Sources

Benjamin O. Foster, Alfred C. Schlesinger, and Russel M. Geer. *Livy: With an English Translation.* Cambridge, Mass: Harvard University Press, 1967.

Paton, W. R., Polybius. *The Histories.* Cambridge: Harvard University Press, 1954.

Selincourt A. De, and Betty Radice. *The War with Hannibal: Books Xxi-Xxx of the History of Rome from Its Foundation.* Baltimore: Penguin Books, 1965.

Secondary Sources

Chaplin, Jane D. *Livy's Exemplary History.* Oxford University Press, 2000.

Davies, Jason P. *Rome's Religious History: Livy, Tacitus, and Ammianus on Their Gods.* Cambridge, UK: Cambridge University Press, 2004.

Glare, P G. W. *Oxford Latin Dictionary.* Oxford Clarendon Press, 1982.

Kajanto, Iiro. *God and Fate in Livy.* Turku: Turun Yliopiston Kustantama, 1957.

Levene, D S. *Religion in Livy.* Leiden: E.J. Brill, 1993.

Patch, Howard R. *The Tradition of the Goddess Fortuna in Roman Literature and the Transitional Period.* Northampton, Mass: Smith College, 1922.

Simpson, D P. *Cassell's New Latin Dictionary: Latin-English, English-Latin.* New York: Funk & Wagnalls, 1960.

Walsh, P G. *Livy: His Historical Aims and Methods.* Cambridge University Press, 1961.

Color and Chains:
Alexis de Tocqueville's Apprehension towards Slavery in Democracy in America

Benjamin Simington

Alexis de Tocqueville writes, "These objects, which touch on my subject, do not enter to it; they are American without being democratic, and it is above all democracy that I wanted to portray" (303). The objects Tocqueville speaks of are the people that inhabit the American Republic, specifically the Indians and Blacks. The latter and their bondage in the institution of American slavery are striking to Tocqueville. The peculiar institution of slavery is unique to Tocqueville and he fears it due to what distinguishes it from the slavery in antiquity: the possibility that blacks in America will never gain equality, and the powder keg that is slavery in the South.

Tocqueville expounds upon the hallmarks of slavery in the ancient world and in the modern world, conveying what is to fear from it. Tocqueville writes, "Among the ancients, the slave belonged to the same race as his master, and often he was superior to him in education and enlightenment" (327). Slavery in antiquity was more egalitarian. This is not present in modern American slavery because the slave was forbidden to read or write (347). The prospect of American slavery forbids knowledge, imprisoning the slave's mind, because it could have brought him to equal footing with his master and thus to freedom. This is frightful to

Tocqueville because the slaves' perpetual ignorance could result in a permanent oppression of a member of the human family. Tocqueville explains that there is predisposition in humans to view the former slave with disdain, but in the ancient world this view was more fleeting due to their overwhelmingly similarity in appearance (327). However, the most deleterious effect of modern American slavery is that the disdain is continual because of the difference of race. Tocqueville writes, "Thus the Negro transmits to all his descendants, with their existence, the external sign of his ignominy" (327). Each of the slave's descendants is constrained because of race in a cyclical manner. Tocqueville expresses consternation towards slavery being connected to something as tangible as race because the notion of inferiority can easily be embedded in American culture, resulting in perpetual disdain towards blacks in America.

Tocqueville observes and fears the idea of color prejudice from slavery is connected to the possible idea that blacks may never be achieve equality in the American Republic. Part of the difficulty in removing the disdain towards color in America is in the nature of democracy. Tocqueville writes, "a whole people cannot thus put itself above itself" (342). Because the American citizens' notions are rooted in popular opinion, popular opinion cannot divorce itself from the collective and step back and analyze its prejudices. If the Americans had an autocratic ruler, perhaps they could be led away from detesting their former slaves, but this is not possible within the confines of democracy (342). The nature of mind and opinion as rooted in the public is inherent in Democracy, so these notions may go on ad infinitum.

Tocqueville fears the extent of racial prejudice in various portions of the country. He writes, "Racial prejudice appears to me stronger in the states that have abolished slavery than in those where slavery still exists, and nowhere it is shown to be as intolerant as in states where servitude has always been unknown" (329). Despite the actual end of slavery in colonies, sharp racial discrimination is still faced by blacks. He is aghast at the fact that although blacks are told they are free, they are not afforded with the same rights and are met with discrimination at every turn. The extent of the denial of his rights, in the form of racial prejudice, is disconcerting

American slavery frightens Tocqueville in the powder keg that represents in the American South. Tocqueville writes, "the hope of freedom had been placed in the bosom of slavery in order to make its rigor milder" (347). So in order to ameliorate the slave's misery, freedom is dangled like a carrot on a string before a rabbit. However, the slaves' hope for freedom combined with their wretchedness makes for a volatile compound. Tocqueville is dismayed by these prospects and foresees them erupting in slave revolts. The greatest instability of American Slavery is inherent in its nature. When the Europeans chose to engage in slavery on the basis of races, they not only thought of it as eternal, but also created a dichotomy between equality and absolute servitude (348). This lack of a middle ground means slavery has to address the humanity of the slave or it will have to come to an inexorable end. Tocqueville reflects this in one of his final statements. Tocqueville writes, "It will cease by the deed of the slave or the master. In both cases, one must expect great misfortunes" (348). Thus, he sees this wretched institution as instability culminating in conflict.

The peculiar institution of slavery is unique to Tocqueville and he fears it due to what distinguishes it from the slavery in the ancient world: the possibility that blacks in America will never gain equal standing, and the powder keg that is slavery in the South. Tocqueville provides probing insight into this peculiar institution and foreshadows the problems that factor into the American Civil War.

The Subjectivity of Morality and Hierarchical Nobility

Jesse Johanning

Throughout the classic short stories in Giovanni Boccaccio's book, *The Decameron,* one will find tediously composed, farcical stories of the shortcomings and triumphs of individuals, whether they are respectable, depraved, commoners or royalty in renaissance era Europe. On the surface, they seem to flirt with the reader in a good natured, almost accidental manner through how they are composed, yet below the surface, humor is merely the language to which Boccaccio uses to convey very perceptive and caustic messages about the idiosyncrasies and paradoxes within societal dynamics of the time. One story in particular that comes to mind when discussing this dimension of Boccaccio's work is Day 2: Story 3 of *The Decameron,* where the author presents a story about three fatally spendthrift brothers who furnish a high interest loan business in England (subsequently taken over by their nephew, Alessandro) in order to restore the foolishly spent fortune they inherited from their father. After civil war erupts in England, the brothers run out of money and are sent to debtor's prison. However on his journey back to Florence from England, Alessandro encounters a person whom he is lead to believe is an abbot traveling to Rome. After getting into bed with this person, he finds that the abbot is really a woman and marries her on a whim. She turns out to be the princess of England, traveling to Rome in order to have her engagement to the King of Scotland relinquished. After gaining approval for their marriage, the couple subsequently frees the brothers from debtor's prison and return to England. Later on, Alessandro becomes the Earl of Cornwall and later the King of Scotland. The central concern of this story is not simply to tell an ironic tale involving a twist of fate, but to confront and expose the real subjectivity of nobility and moral constructs.

The story is prefaced with a testimonial personifying the nature of fortune; Pampinea states that, "it is [fortune] who, according to her own *secret judgment*, endlessly moves and rearranges things from one place to another and then back again without any discernible plan whatsoever" (Boccaccio, 86). In the context of this story, it appears on the surface that Boccaccio is wishing to tell a humorous tale about people doing iniquitous things followed by unsuitably good fortune. I would argue that their consequences, conversely, are far from unexpected. In the previously mentioned quote, a vital word to note is "judgment." Judgment, in this case, seems to have a dual meaning. It refers to fortune's judgment relating to her arrangement of events as well as her judgment of the characters' actions. Because the story is prefaced with a statement relating fortune to judgment, we can safely detect the author's intentions to relate the actions in the story to their consequences and/or rewards based on their perceived morality. The writer's choice to use the word "fortune" rather than "God" is also noteworthy in the case of discussing a transcendent entity observing/judging man's exploits and controlling the outcome of events. Perhaps Boccaccio does this intentionally in order to avoid the accusation that he is trying to say that God permits the illustrated actions in this story. For example, Alessandro gets in bed with someone whom he thinks is an Abbot and ends up being rewarded with wealth and nobility. It could be argued that the characters are only rewarded based on an indeterministic quality that might be assigned to fortune. Yet, we know that Boccaccio is not wishing to state that fortune is unaffected by the deeds of men because not only does he state that his personified fortune makes judgment, but also "moves and rearranges" things in accordance to this judgment.

In order to see how Boccaccio views nobility, it is important to observe the actions and motivations of the character who ultimately becomes the Earl of Cornwall and later the King of Scotland–Alessandro. The first thing we notice is that nearly all of his actions are motivated by greed. For instance, Alessandro's decision to aid in his uncles' high interest loan company (87) is a perfect example. The business of high interest loaning was not looked upon favorably at this time. Dante's *The Inferno*, which condemns usury (Canto XI), was published less than 50 years prior to the publication of *The Decameron*. If Alessandro were a pious man, he would not take this job. Yet, he does so (87) with no evidence of reluctance. For this business move, Alessandro is greatly rewarded and we know that monetary greed is a primary motivation for him. Later on, he begins to make riskier and more lucrative loans by his own accord and not by the brothers' request. This demonstrates that he makes decisions based on satisfying his own desires and not simply bowing to authority (his brothers). "[Alessandro] had begun to loan money to barons on the security of their castles and other revenues, which brought him in a handsome profit" (87). Boccaccio makes no mention that the brothers also benefit from this business strategy – only Alessandro. One might argue that Alessandro is punished, for, in the midst of the civil war, the company goes under and he has to travel back to Italy. This is actually more of a temporary financial sacrifice than an authentic punishment. The reason why is because the King's turbulent relationship with his son (which catalyzed the civil war) provides the opportunity for Alessandro's ascent in reputation when he resolves their issues and gains mass fame and admiration throughout England (93).

One might argue that the brothers' own greed brings them punishment when they are thrown into debtor's prison. However, it is only by the brothers' own lack of adaptability that punishment materializes. "On the other hand, the three brothers went on spending excessively, borrowing more and more money every day, but as the years passed, they realized their hopes were without foundation" (88). Their persistent frivolous spending and naivety is what places them in prison (88), not their greed. The brothers' greed is what catalyzes the foundation of their high interest loan company -the source of their fortune. Their unwillingness to adapt to circumstances and lack of foresight brings them misfortune.

Being thrown into debtor's prison, however, is very transitory in the overall scheme of the story, for in the end, the brothers are set free and live fruitful lives (93).

By the end of the story, Alessandro receives one of the greatest rewards/honors that one could hope for – kinghood (94). However, the opportunities that he opens for himself in becoming the Earl of Cornwall (94) are aided not by his nobility, but through acting on his carnal desires. For example, at the inn, we find Alessandro and the Abbot in a bedroom. The Abbot observes Alessandro and deliberates. "Determined to take advantage of [the situation], the Abbot waited until all was completely quiet in the inn and then in a low voice he called Alessandro and told him to lie down beside him. After many a polite refusal, Alessandro undressed and did so" (90). At the time, Alessandro does not know that the Abbot is really a woman, much less an English Princess. Despite Alessandro's hesitance, we know he is eager and willing to get intimate with the Abbot since Alessandro undresses himself on his own accord. After their hasty marriage, it is clear that Alessandro's choice to have sex with the Abbot/Princess produced favorable results when Alessandro finds out that the Abbot is really an English Princess (91). Had he been pious and refused to get in bed with the Abbot, he would have lost the princess's marriage proposal and his brothers would still be in jail. The following actions in the Princess's bed prove to be just as crucial to Alessandro's good fortune. Upon revealing that she is really a woman (91), she expounds this to Alessandro: "I fell so much in love with you (Alessandro) when I saw you... For this reason I have decided to take you as my husband over all other men" (91). Without much hesitation, Alessandro agrees. The chief difference between this act and his previous advancement on the woman is that his motivations have shifted from lust back to greed. One may argue that Alessandro's acceptance to the proposal is merely a case of him succumbing to someone else's demands, since she gives him an ultimatum, "if you do not wish to take me as your wife, leave here immediately and return to where you were" (91). However, we see that Alessandro does not even consider the ultimatum when deliberating on the proposal. "Although Alessandro knew nothing about her, he judged from the company she kept that she must be noble and wealthy, and he could see for himself that she was very beautiful. So without giving the matter another thought, he replied that if the arrangement please her, it was certainly most pleasing to him" (91). Because Alessandro's reasoning for this hasty life decision of marriage is solely based on her appearance of affluence and beauty, one can safely assume that greed and lust are his primary motivations. He is, unmistakably, only thinking about the financial and lustful gain he may inherit rather than the possible punishment he may receive if he doesn't accept the proposal. This impulse on the foundations of greed clearly ends up paying off when they reach the Vatican to speak with the Pope. Alessandro does not know that the woman is a princess until this point. In speaking of her arranged marriage, the woman reveals that she has "fled in secret, taking with [her] a large part of the treasures belonging to [her] father, the King of England, who planned to have [her] marry the King of Scotland..." (92). Needless to say, had Alessandro chosen the path of piety, his chances of marrying into nobility would have been nearly nonexistent.

Boccaccio is not trying to prove that profane pursuits alone constitute any form of success, nobility or power. We know that Boccaccio is not trying to say this because the brothers, who appear to be motivated solely by greed, do not encounter the same fortune as Alessandro. We also know that Alessandro is not merely a two-dimensional wanton, solely fixated on satisfying his lust and monetary greed. This is proven by the deed he commits that brings him national celebration. "Alessandro was clever and skillful enough to reconcile the King with his son, which was most beneficial to the entire island, and in so doing he won the love and favor of all its inhabitants;" (94) The real reason why Alessandro succeeds in gaining these opportunities for sex, money, and nobility is through his skill, cleverness and appearance of nobility through his eloquence. His motivation is also not out of good will. We know that Alessandro has demonstrated ample foresight to see how reuniting England will help his reputation. Boccaccio demonstrates that it is not through chastity, piety, or even caution that one finds them in power or nobility, but through social skill combined with the aptness to act on one's carnal desires. Another crucial piece in this puzzle is that it is actually Alessandro's *appearance* of nobility and class that gives him the opportunities he has. The King only approves of Alessandro's marriage to his daughter because of two knights that vouch for him because "his appearance and manners made him seem more like a man of royal blood than one who loaned money as a profession" (93).

One might assert that Boccaccio is still trying to claim that those of nobility and power really are in their positions due to their moral upstanding –and Alessandro just tricked them. This is not true. Alessandro truly has achieved genuine nobility through his ignoble pursuits. The King of England seeks for his daughter to hold a marriage with the King of Scotland, (92) presumably for political reasons. The princess intentionally seeks Alessandro out as a husband instead based on perceivably ignoble lust on both ends. "At first glance, [Alessandro] pleased the Abbot more than anything else had ever pleased [her] before" (89). Alessandro rises to the Earl of Cornwall through these pursuits motivated by greed and lust (as previously explicated). Upon reaching Earldom, Alessandro later rises to become the King of Scotland. This is what the King of England wanted all along –for his daughter to marry the King of Scotland. Alessandro has now fulfilled every expectation the King had for a noble son-in-law. Not only has Alessandro achieved this Kinghood, but he has worked to win the King of England's favor (through impressing the knights as well as reuniting the King with his son); something the former King of Scotland may not have worked as hard to do. Of course, the King's initial approval was only important to Alessandro so he could marry his daughter. The reuniting of the King and his son was also motivated by Alessandro's own pursuit of glory, as previously expounded. Nevertheless, Alessandro is rendered genuinely noble through his selfish and ignoble motivations because he has satisfied all of the expectations that the King and Princess have for noble family. When closely observed, the line between a greedy, self-serving man and a man of great nobility is blurred almost beyond recognition in this story. In this observation, we can perceive actual the subjectivity of hierarchical nobility and moral constructs.

The reason why this message is hidden rather than stated bluntly could be because Boccaccio deems this advice only to be helpful to those who are intelligent enough to pursue this path "properly." If everybody was motivated to travel through life in this fashion, it would surely be a disaster – for it is much more important that the masses follow basic moral constructs in order to achieve a more steady harmony. All the stories on Day 2 of the book have a reoccurring theme of "unexpected plot twists." The reason why he writes this story in the day whose theme is unexpected plot twists is to convey the idea that the common people should not be jealous or get down on themselves because of the success and power of some because those few most likely got there through immoral actions (that are likely to be punishable in the afterlife!). The rewards in this story simply seem counter-intuitive and thus unexpected for the general public that views morality and reward as a simple economy of getting what you pay for.

We know that this message is especially important to Boccaccio because Pampinea is the character responsible for the telling of this story. From the beginning, she is depicted as being the leader. She is the person responsible for bringing the entire group and out to the country. She also proclaims herself to be the queen of the group on the first day, whereas we do not observe any assertive actions like this from any of the other characters. On top of that, the importance of the characters in Pampinea's actual story should be taken into account in regards to punishment and reward as well.

Alessandro is the only real *character* in this tale. This is because he is the only one that is named - apart from Agolanti. The only reason why Agolanti is named is to draw a connection with the historical Agolanti family - the real life bankers - and how they were rewarded when England actually erupted in civil war. The brothers are unnamed, so we can infer that, by the same reasoning unnamed characters are portrayed in parables, they symbolize people who acts on their desires without skill or foresight. The king and princess simply serve as symbols for nobility.

The King of England seeks for his daughter to hold relations with the King of Scotland, presumably for political reasons (92). The princess intentionally seeks Alessandro out as a husband based on perceived ignoble lust. "At first glance, [Alessandro] pleased the Abbot more than anything else had ever pleased [her] before" (89). Alessandro rises to the Earl of Cornwall through his pursuits motivated by greed and lust (as previously explicated). The King approves of Alessandro's marriage to his daughter because of two knights that vouch for him because "his *appearance* and *manners* made him seem more like a man of royal blood than one who loaned money as a profession" (93). Alessandro later rises to become the King of Scotland. This is what the King of England wanted all along – for his daughter to marry the King of Scotland. Alessandro has become genuinely noble through all of his ignoble deeds. We can perceive the subjectivity of hierarchical nobility and moral constructs because an extremely ignoble man can be easily mistaken for someone on the opposite end of the spectrum.

Not only does Giovanni Boccaccio wish to convey this certain flaw, or at the very least, idiosyncrasy in societal undercurrents and operations, but through his choice of the character he decides to tell the story through, it is observable that this message is particularly dear to his heart. He is showing the reflective reader the power that superficial appearance of virtue and quality have in any given society or conglomerate of human interactions. In terms of reciprocal moral interaction versus reward, what sets Alessandro apart from the other characters in this story was certainly not his nobility but his *surface appearance* of nobility. The central concern of this story is not simply to tell an ironic tale involving a twist of fate, but to expose the real subjectivity of nobility and moral constructs as well as its vitality in society being grounded almost entirely on a superficial level.

Faulkner: Pride, Duty, and Family

Alyssa Miller

To be Southern is to host a whole range of stereotypes, criticisms, and assumptions. It is to be blamed for slavery, to be on the losing side of the Civil War. In the North, Southerners are thought to be stupid, backwards, uneducated. However, there is also an innate notion of Southern comfort and Southern hospitality. There is the endearing Southern twang, with images of a kindly, plump mother cooking dinner for her family, of neighbors who are actually neighborly, and of a life where virtues are unquestioningly upheld. The South encompasses these thoughts, images, ideas, and more - and William Faulkner wrote about them all. Faulkner, perhaps more than any other author, explored all of the intricacies and depths of this unique niche of the world. What he seems to have found is a series of contradictions and ambiguities. Southern values - pride, duty, and family - can be both admirable and repugnant. Faulkner respects the nobility of these Southern ideals, while simultaneously questioning their value.

Faulkner's "The Tall Men" exalts the purity of heart promoted by Southern ideology. In the story, a government investigator is sent to collect two brothers who have ignored their summons to register for the draft. The investigator hates these country people,

"These people who lie about... [who] make false statements to get seed loans which they will later misuse... Government asks one thing of them in return, one thing simply, which is to put their names down on a selective-service list, they refuse to do it" (46).

He is outraged at these farmers who are being given government relief, and just knows that they are abusing it. He knows that they are crafty, self-serving, and ungrateful. He repeats the phrase, again and again, *"These people"* – they are the other, the lower, the leeches of society. When he finds that the marshal has called the house to say that they are coming for the boys, he is outraged, believing that the boys will have fled long before he has the chance to incarcerate them.

Upon arriving at the house, however, the investigator finds that the boys have not fled. Instead, the whole family surrounds their father's sickbed as the doctor tends his mutilated leg. The family does not understand why the boys would have needed to register. The question that is asked over and over is, "You mean we have declared war?" (47). This is a family who will gladly take up arms to fight for their country – the elder men have already, honorably, done so. Without a war, though, they do not understand why they would need to register. It just doesn't make sense. At the appearance of the investigator, though, despite his confusion, the wounded man tells his sons to go. "'This gentleman has come all the way from Jackson to say the Government is ready for you. I reckon the quickest place to enlist will be Memphis. Go upstairs and pack.,'" he orders them. Without hesitation the boys obey, despite their father lying, possibly dying, on the table. They pack and they leave for Memphis.

The investigator, of course, believes the boys are registering in an attempt to evade arrest. He simply cannot see the pure-heartedness of this family, who are so duty and family bound that they will do whatever is right, no matter the cost. The marshal becomes the sage-like spokesperson for the family, and for the Southern country people. He quietly and politely chats about the family that the investigator so obviously despises. He tells the investigator the history of this family, riddled with honor and pride in their country. Most importantly however, he tells the investigator that this family never wanted government subsidies. "They just couldn't believe that the Government aimed to help a man whether he wanted help or not" (56). They believed that a person needed to either succeed or fail on their own merits, and they refused government aide year in and year out. The marshal, kindly looking down on the investigator, explains: "'We done invented ourselves so many alphabets and rules and recipes that we can't see anything else... We have slipped our backbone" (59). The new world is so ignorant, so restricting, that true honor, pride, and duty – the backbone, the strength of humanity – exists only in these simple Southern people. As the marshal, the sage, the wise speaker of truth, tells the investigator: "Life has got cheap, and life ain't cheap... I don't mean just getting from one WPA relief check to the next one, but honor and pride and discipline that make a man worth preserving, make him of any value" (60).

In "The Tall Men" classic Southern ideals are at the heart of morality. They are what "make [a man] of any value" (60). "The Tall Men" shows the Southern man at his best. In "A Rose for Emily" however, Faulkner gives a vastly different depiction of pride and family. Miss Emily Grierson, the title character, is the manifestation of the Old South, the pre-Civil War South, in a new and modern age. In this new age, the morals and ideals of the former, presumably morally superior era are being changed and shifted. Virtually every image, from the description of Emily's house to her person, shows the decay of this old, golden age. Her neighborhood has been "encroached and obliterated," leaving only her house standing, "lifting its stubborn and coquettish decay above the cotton wagons... an eyesore among eyesores" (119). Of Emily, "Her skeleton was small and spare... She looked bloated, like a body long submerged in motionless water, and of that pallid hue" (121). It is as though she and her house were already dead while she was alive. It is as though the old traditions, the old values of the South were already dead.

Of these old Southern morals, the one that Emily and the Griersons represent best is pride. The town speaks of the Griersons as the most prideful, arrogant family in existence. And the town despises them for it. When Emily's father died and she was left near penniless and without husband, the town was satisfied that she would be forced to recognize her new social position. Instead, though, "She carried her head high enough – even when we believed that she was fallen. It was as if she demanded more than ever the recognition of her dignity as the last Grierson" (125). Still, without any of her former status, Emily is full of fiery pride – the true Grierson pride, the same pride that her father felt when rejecting any offers of marriage for Emily, knowing that nobody was good enough to marry *his* daughter.

In the end of the story, we find that Emily has murdered the only suitor she ever had after the death of her father. Though it is not specified in the story, it can be inferred that she loved the man, but he did not want to marry her. So she kills him. Moreover, we find that she has been living with, and sleeping with, his corpse. The man's dead body has been acting as her living husband. Faulkner treats her insanity with both a morbid humor and profound sense of sadness, almost pity. In the middle of the dust and decay of her boarded-up upstairs bedroom, "The man himself lay in the bed" (130). It is a single line – its own paragraph – shocking and horrifying the reader. The man has a "profound fleshless grin," and appears to have once lain "in the attitude of an embrace" (130). Faulkner plays with images such as these, and states them so matter-of-factly, that they draw a kind of bewildered, disgusted amusement at the implications.

Emily, despite her murderous act and blatant insanity, is a sympathetic character. Faulkner goes to great pains to paint a portrait of her childhood, almost literally:

> "We had long thought of them as a tableau, Miss Emily a slender figure in white in the background, her father a spraddled silhouette in the foreground, his back to her and

clutching a horsewhip, the two of them framed by the back-flung front door" (123).

Emily, as a young woman, is a "slender figure in white", (an obvious symbols for a pure, innocent young woman,) forced into the background by her domineering, tyrannical father. Her father's pride oppressed her, keeping her from suitors, and therefore from love. When her father dies, the town understands her refusal to admit that he is dead because, as they put it, "We remembered all the young men her father had driven away, and we knew that with nothing left, she would have to cling to that which had robbed her, as people will" (124). This is the first hint at her madness, and at its cause. Her family and their Grierson pride have left her with nothing but an empty house and a sense of entitlement. She is sympathetic because it is that old Southern pride that has led her to a life of misery and the madness of being alone.

In "A Rose for Emily," pride is a hurtful value, not only for the members of the Grierson family, but to everyone around them. There is none of the reverence for pride, duty, and family as in "The Tall Men." In yet another story, "Hair," Faulkner explores both the nobility and the personal harm of duty and family. The main character, Hawkshaw is a barber. In the beginning of the story, we find that the town is concerned with his seemingly unhealthy fascination with a young orphan girl. She is the only person that Hawksaw has ever shown any affection for. When she passes the barber shop on her way to school, Hawksaw stares out the window at her. He gives her presents every Christmas, and insists on serving her whenever she comes into the shop. And so, the years pass. Soon, she is a young, promiscuous woman. And yet, Hawksaw does not appear to be one of her lovers. Instead, he buys her a sixty dollar watch and then does not give it to her for over two years because "he thinks she is too young to receive jewelry from anybody that aint kin to her" (136). His affection appears to be asexual and gentlemanly, despite its abnormality.

As the story progresses, we learn that Hawksaw, (or Henry Stribling, his real name,) was once married to a woman who looked remarkably like the girl he is so partial to. Henry had been a hardworking man, who fell in love with a woman slightly above his station and worked hard for the right to marry her. When the woman's father died, Henry spent all of the money he had saved for a mortgage on a funeral for the man, and was forced to start saving again. Then, before the couple could even have a wedding, the woman got very sick. Her last words were: "Take care of maw. The mortgage. Paw wont like it to be left so. Send for Henry." repeated over and over. And so, she died, and Henry unquestioningly does exactly as he was bid. He leaves town, but continues to pay off the mortgage. Every year, he returns to his beloved's home to clean and tend the house and the yard, and to check on her mother. Finally, the mother dies too. And yet, Henry continues to care for the house and pay off the mortgage. When the narrator visits the house, "It was as clean as a hospital. The stove was polished and the woodbox filled," even though nobody lives there (146). His sense of duty is remarkably sweet. In the house, "The wedding license was framed, hanging above the mantel like a picture," there because it is the only remnant of his dear wife, whose only photograph and lock of hair were lost (146).

Hawksaw could easily have abandoned the house and his wife's mother. Then, when the mother died, he could have even more easily abandoned just the house, which was destined to be claimed by distant relatives as soon as the mortgage was paid. Nobody would have blamed him. However, out of love and duty towards his wife's last wishes, he does not. Really, the whole venture is pointless, worthless to him. He is feeding his earnings into something that he will never own, and his obligation leaves him withdrawn, living a secret second life. It is not until his obligation is fulfilled and the mortgage is paid that he is able to move on. He marries that girl that he used to watch from the barbershop window, and is able to continue living the life that he lost when his wife died. In the meantime, though, he lost twenty-five years of his life to secrecy and sorrow because of his duty and obligation.

In "Hair," Faulkner still appears to hold Southern values in some sort of esteem, despite their potential for harm. "Barn Burning," though, is the ultimate criticism of pride, duty, and family. "Barn Burning" is a heart-wrenching tale about a child who finds himself irrevocably bound to his vile father. Snopes, the father, has a deep-seeded hatred and resentment towards his position in society: he is of the lowest white class, and is destined to work as a sharecropper in a post-slavery South. At least when slavery existed, he was certain that there was a class of people below himself. Now, however, the freed blacks are a personal affront to his pride. Refusing to admit his station, he acts as though he is above all authority, showing his arrogance and bloated sense of self by intentionally disrespecting anyone who dares to be of a higher class, then burning down their barn when they attempt to bring him to justice. The boy in the story, Colonel Sartoris (or Sarty), finds himself morally conflicted by his father. When brought before the judge after the first barn burning in the story, the boy realizes that the victim is not only his father's enemy, but "*our enemy* he thought in that despair; *ourn! Mine and hisn both! He's my father!*" (3). The knowledge that this man is his father is striking, almost surprising, and the knowledge that his father's enemies are his enemies is deeply upsetting and unfair, though unequivocal. His sense of duty towards his father is palpable and distressing; it is so substantial that he can smell it as well as the food that his hungry stomach craves: "the smell and sense just a little of fear because mostly of despair and grief, the old fierce pull of blood" (3). His relationship is a source of "despair and grief," but for some reason that the boy cannot seem to explain, the blood in his veins creates an ancient, familial obligation to his father – no matter how horrible a man he is.

Sarty has faced this wretched ambivalence all his life: the belief that he must support his blood kin, and the knowledge that his father is wrong. At a young age, he has been faced with moral ambiguity again and again, and it torments him. With the innocence of a young child, when the family moves again and finds itself working for an incredibly rich family, the boy dreamily thinks:

> *They are safe from him. People whose lives are a part of this peace and dignity are beyond his touch, he no more to them than a buzzing wasp: capable of stinging for a moment but that's all...*

The house, in all its extravagance, exudes an impenetrability that the boy believes even Snopes will have to recognize and respect. He continues, again and again, to hope that his father is done, that perhaps the family can live in peace. The beauty of this house, however, proves to have the opposite effect. Snopes, in seeing a life that he can never hope to achieve, fills with resentment, despising these people who think that they are better than him. Approaching the door of the mansion, Snopes intentionally drags his foot through horse shit, preparing to show exactly what he thinks of this upper class. When the door is answered by a black servant, who dares order Snopes to wipe his foot, Snopes is even more incensed. He walks through the room, destroying an expensive white rug. The boy, watches, mortified. The whole scene gives the sense of occurring in slow-motion, as "the boy watched him pivot on the good leg and saw the stiff foot drag round the arc of the turning, leaving a final long and fading smear" (12). Upon leaving, Snopes tells his son: "'Pretty and white, ain't it? ... That's sweat. Nigger sweat. Maybe it ain't white enough yet to suit him. Maybe he wants to mix some white sweat with it" (12).

His pride is livid that he is now virtually of the same class as the blacks.

Snopes' pride continues to hurt his family. When the rug is brought to them to be cleaned, he intentionally ruins it. When the owner of the mansion tells him he will dock his pay to make up for it, Snopes goes to the courthouse to sue him. All the while, the boy maintains his hope: "*Maybe it will all add up and balance and vanish - corn, rug, fire; the terror and grief, the being pulled two ways like between two teams of horses - gone, done with for ever and ever*" (17). He is hoping for some miracle, some possibility for a different life. He thinks of the battle between his duty to his father and his morality as being "pulled two ways like between two teams of horses;" it is an impossible strain that feels as though it could kill him.

Sarty's hopes are, of course, unfounded. Just as he has always done, Snopes decides to punish the rich for being rich. Sarty hears his mother's voice: "'Abner! No! No! Oh, God. Oh, God. Abner!" - setting the terrifying, helpless, desperate scene (20). Abner Snopes orders his son to go get him the can of oil from the barn, and Sarty runs for the stable, "this the old habit, the old blood which he had not been permitted to choose for himself, which had been bequeathed him willy nilly" (21). He obeys his father because it is his father. He is duty-bound to those who share his blood, even though it was "bequeathed him willy nilly," without thought, reason, or explanation. As he runs, he thinks, "*I could run on and on and never look back, never need to see his face again. Only I can't. I can't*" (21). As Snopes leaves, he orders the mother to hold onto Sarty, to make sure he does not go and warn the owners of the mansion. As he begs his mother to let him go, his mother responds with the same cold sense of reluctant obligation that Sarty has experienced all his life: "'Don't you see I can't?'" (22).

Sarty escapes his mother's grasp, and runs to the big white house. He bursts into the house, yelling "Barn!" and runs away before they can catch him. And he keeps running, "knowing it was too late yet still running even after he heard the shot and, an instant later two shots, pausing now without knowing he had ceased to run, crying 'Pap! Pap!'" (24). He is running away from his life, away from his father and his blood obligation. Now, his father dead and he mourns. "*Father. My father*, he thought," still constantly reminding himself of his duty: now, of his duty to mourn. He sleeps, without realizing it, on the ground. He wakes up cold and stiff, "but walking would cure that... and soon there would be the sun" (25). Walking and moving forwards now that he is able to, now that his father is dead, will cure all. The sun will rise again, and the future is hopeful and full of light. Now that his father is dead, he is free from all of that horrifying, terrifying pride, that disgusting, destructive duty. He walks on, and "He [does] not look back" (25).

Faulkner's South is filled with ambiguities. The question does not appear to be whether the South holds pride, duty, and family as staples of morality, but rather whether it should. The family in "The Tall Men" represents the very best of these ideals; its members are good, and kind, and honorable. They are full of pride for their hard work: so much so that they refuse government aide, believing that men should fend for themselves. The Griersons, however, in "A Rose for Emily," are full of a disdainful pride that separates them from the rest of their community and ultimately drives Miss Emily crazy. Family, for the Griersons, is an oppressive institution. Henry in "Hair" is an honorable man, fulfilling his wife's wishes long after her death. However, his sense of duty and family lead him to waste twenty-five years of his life. Finally, Snopes' pride and Sarty's familial duty in "Barn Burning" destroy them. Snopes lives a life full of hatred, ruining his family's lives, while Sarty finds himself emotionally wrecked by the moral ambivalence, and by his desire to be good in a world where he is obligated not to be. Faulkner explores the intricacies of humanity in the Southern world and ultimately concludes nothing regarding these three virtues. Nothing, except that there is nothing to conclude. It is not these virtues that are either right or wrong – it is the people that are either right or wrong. People can uphold these virtues morally or immorally, they can be right, wrong, or in between. Pride, duty, and family may hurt if people let them, or they may be the utmost channels for human virtue. Faulkner's great achievement is allowing us to experience humanity from all ends, and elucidating the great ambiguities and conflicts in human nature.

Berger and the Nude

Emily Ramirez

In early European art, women were objectified through the depiction of them as passive while presenting themselves in a way to be judged on their appearance. This was seen even before the Renaissance, in the Ancient Grecian sculpture of "Kore in Sleeved Chiton" (Chios, Greece, c. 525 B.C.E.). The subject of the sculpture is a woman who is ornamented in finery and whose facial expression is that of serenity. This idea of women was extended and blossomed in European oil paintings of the early Renaissance, coinciding with the emergence of the female nude.

Berger offers several historical factors that could have led to the abundant imagery of the female nude in European oil paintings. First and foremost, there is a significant distinction between nakedness and a nude figure. While being naked is simply being without clothing, a "naked body has to be seen as an object in order to become a nude" (Berger 54). This means that a nude is a body that has been objectified and put on display for the viewing pleasure of others. Berger says that women are born into the hands of men and that the social standing of women is of being property to men. This causes women to become passive and to view themselves as objects. Religious beliefs also played a large role in how women were viewed during the Renaissance. In fact, the first nudes in European paintings portrayed the story of Adam and Eve in the Garden of Eden. Because a woman was the original source of sin, the Bible says that women are punished by being made subservient to men. Essentially, the inferiority that women faced in society due to these historical factors made them easy targets for objectification in art.

As nudes became a popular art form, these paintings began to depict secular scenes and conventions were developed. By convention, the nudes in European paintings are always women. Men may be pictured, but the focal point is always upon the female. However, the protagonist is not the female; the protagonist is assumed to be a male outside of the painting who is the viewer. The fact that the female subject of the painting is naked is a sign of submission to the desires of the male viewer, which is why almost all female nudes have signs of passivity in their expression and posture. For this reason, the convention of the female subject portrayed from a frontal view is seen, such as in "Allegory of Time and Love" by Bronzino. The woman, Venus, while kissing Cupid, isn't shown in relation to Cupid. She is shown from a frontal view as a display for the pleasure of the male viewer. Berger confirms this in his claim that, "This picture is made to appeal to *his* sexuality. It has nothing to do with her sexuality," (55). Another convention – that of the absence of hair on women's bodies – is pictured in Bronzino's painting, as well. Hair has long symbolized the power of women, so the lack thereof as a convention was another way to put the viewer in control of female nudes in paintings.

Other themes prevalent among European oil paintings of nudes include the idea of women being judged, most readily present in depictions of "The Judgment of Paris." The sense that women were to be judged on outward appearance further emphasizes women as objects, rather than human beings. Due to women being judged on appearance, it is logical to assume that women, in turn, were concerned with their appearance. Yet this is criticized rather hypocritically in depictions of "Vanity," where women stare at themselves in mirrors – a symbol of their vanity. Berger suggests that mirrors in these paintings stand for more than vanity. He believes that the true function of mirrors is to, again, relay that women are objects to be seen and nothing more – an idea that permeates through images of female nudes in European Renaissance art

Portia as Playwright:
Education of the Neoplatonic Artisan in *The Merchant of Venice*

Hunter McKenzie

The Merchant of Venice is a thematically rich and emotionally sprawling work. Although it contains the traditional elements of a romantic comedy, it culminates in a dramatic court scene, which treats primarily of justice. Comedy as a whole is a genre characterized by a narrative impetus towards resolution and reconciliation of apparently contradictory desires and loyalties. By expanding his comedy to include discussion of justice and law, Shakespeare encourages the audience to consider whether justice can be romantically, comedically reconciled to other individual and societal needs and concerns, such as love, prosperity, and, at a deeper level, a hope for some shared human good which can transcend economic relationships.

The primary agent of reconciliation and harmonization of these various forces at work in the play is Portia, who takes an active role in constructing her own desired comedic resolution. The apparent stasis and resolution we receive at the end of the play is troubling upon further examination, particularly because of its insufficient treatment of certain problems of justice. Through this experience, Portia comes to realize in the final Belmont garden scene that the essential human struggle is to create not an absolute Neoplatonic good, but a provisional sense of harmony.

This struggle speaks to a shared concern between comedy and tragedy with the possibility of harmony in the world, and the activity of theater as an exploration of this problem.

Although Portia's solution to the problems of the play may prove ultimately problematic, close attention to Portia's speeches throughout *The Merchant of Venice* demonstrate her profound intellectual strength and moral complexity. She is aware of the gap between the imagined or pretended ideal and the reality of human life. Her first lines in the play are "By my troth, Nerissa, my little body is aweary of this great world." (I.ii.1-2) Her opening speech directly follows, and is to be compared and contrasted to the opening lines of Antonio, who opens the play with a perplexed expression of his own sadness. Both speeches betray a sort of melancholy, stemming from a disappointment in the world's failure to satisfy longing for the ideal, and they are delivered by two of the most mysterious and emotionally complex characters in the play.

Portia's first speech is followed by a detailed description of Portia's suitors. This brilliant scene serves several purposes. It makes clear to the audience that Portia is being pursued by rich men from all over the world, and explains the nature of the casket game. Moreover, it exhibits Portia's razor-sharp wit and ironic sense of humor. It also reveals deeper aspects of her character. For instance, when queried regarding the German suitor, she states significantly, "I will do anything, Nerissa, ere I be married to a sponge" (I.ii.96-97). This unequivocal statement suggests that

Portia has a deeper set of values that governs her action. That a drunkard is particularly disgusting to Portia suggests that she despises mental laziness, and values sobriety and engagement with the problems of the world. She does not want merely a husband who will satisfy her father's will, but a companion whose mental faculties are a worthy match to her own. The image of a detached drunkard can be well contrasted against Nerissa's description of Bassanio as "a scholar and a soldier" (I.ii.112).

Another remarkable revelation about Portia in this scene is that she, although disappointed with the nature of the world, is unabashedly aware of the discrepancies between appearance and reality, and can talk about them with eloquence and frankness. Although her suitors are men of nobility, wealth, and influence, she exposes their flaws and falsehoods ruthlessly, refusing to accept the myths of nobility, which they attempt to perpetrate by appearing in pomp and grandeur.

Another contrast that can be made between Antonio's opening statement and Portia's that immediately follows is that the first is delivered in verse, while the exchange between Portia and Nerissa occurs entirely in prose. This is one of few occurrences of prose dialogue throughout the play. Although one possible cause for this switch to prose is that Nerissa is of a lower rank than Portia, it should be noted that Portia and Nerissa converse in verse elsewhere in the play, such as at the end of Act II, Scene ix. This scene therefore stands out. When Portia's sharp, jocular colloquialism is contrasted with Antonio's comparative lyricism, this may suggest that her response to the problems of life is emblematic of a different *approach* to them than his.

Antonio's approach is passive; he sees his sadness as emanating from a cause beyond himself, which he cannot identify. When Portia's active engagement with the problems of reality and lucid prose speech are contrasted against Antonio's passivity and verse, a dichotomy emerges that distinguishes two approaches to life, as represented in literary genres - the tragic and the comic. Tragic characters of the Classical tradition, such as Oedipus and Achilles, fall prey to fate and necessity. The fallen nature of the world is fixed in the order of the cosmos, and attempts to alter it or surpass human limitation end in widespread disaster. Antonio will later willingly play out this tragic approach, accepting his role as a martyr to love for Bassanio (although it can certainly be argued that Antonio does not possess the grandeur and grace of Shakespeare's true tragic heroes). Comedy, however, takes a more flexible approach to the imperfections of life; conflicts can be resolved, oaths can be taken back, the gods can be persuaded, and the lowest beggar can have his day in the sun. The play is a comedy, and so Portia reigns supreme over it, but the elements of potential tragedy, which undermine it, are linked to Antonio. Furthermore, as the foremost representative of comedy in the play, it falls upon Portia to resolve the problems that tragedy creates for itself, to redeem her friends and ultimately her society in a grand harmonic gesture.

It is difficult to determine what values and concerns guide Portia's sense of harmony, sense many of her speeches occur in public or in disguise. However, an examination of her reactions to her various suitors in the first three acts can offer insight into her character. One interesting example is the derision she displays towards Morocco after his selection of the incorrect casket, which Portia refers to as a "gentle riddance" (II.vii.78). She follows by saying "Let all of his complexion choose me so" (II.vii.79). This must not be taken to mean that Portia is simply reacting to Morocco's skin color; this would directly contradict her explicit claim, "In terms of choice I am not solely led/By nice direction of a maiden's eyes" (II.i.14). Furthermore, the word "complexion" has a wider range of meaning for Shakespeare than it commonly does today; for instance, Solanio uses it at III.i.28 to describe the natural behavior of a bird leaving its nest. Portia has disdain not for Morocco's physical appearance but for his behavior as it has been revealed by his actions and speeches in the short time she has known him.

A commonly accepted interpretation of this scene is that she disdains Morocco for being easily deceived by appearances, but this reading is problematic, given that Portia later deliberately deceives Bassanio concerning her very identity, and in fact premises her scheme on the assumption that she will be able to remain unrecognized by him. Afterward she does not indicate that she respects Bassanio any less for having been deceived by her appearance, but rather reprimands him for not having "...defended it/With any terms of zeal..."(V.i.204-205). Portia understands the power of illusion and outward appearance, and has no qualms about using it to her advantage. Morocco, however, betrays another trait that makes him, by her estimation, unfit to marry her. He laments that he must choose among the caskets, saying,

> But alas the while,
> If Hercules and Lichas play at dice
> Which is the better man, the greater throw
> May turn by fortune from the weaker hand.
> So is Alcides beaten by his page,
> And so may I, blind Fortune leading me,
> Miss that which one unworthier may attain... (II.i.31-37)

In this passage Morocco, in addition to plainly displaying a rather arrogant confidence in his manly worthiness, emphasizes several times that he sees the selection of the caskets purely as a game of chance. It does not occur to him to consider that he is undertaking a test of his wits. Even after having read the caskets, he apparently does not at first perceive that the inscriptions are riddles, for he says "Some god direct my judgment! Let me see— /I will survey th' inscriptions back again" (II.vii.13-14). Because he does not recognize that his prudence and wisdom are being evaluated, the casket game must be decided for Morocco by chance, or by his fancy, which is drawn immediately to the gold (II.vii.4). From the very beginning this disqualifies him from being a worthy husband for Portia, both because it suggests an underlying intellectual laziness, and because it reveals that he regards fortune passively, as an uncontrollable force that is leading him. Portia, on the other hand, will take an active hand in sculpting her own fate.

When she is later being courted by Bassanio, Portia's statements suggest that she is also seriously concerned with preserving a value in human relationships higher than the simply economic, and that she considers her risk of marrying someone like Morocco or Aragon to have an important resonance for the world beyond her. Portia reiterates the significance of her plight to Bassanio with a grandiose reference to Greek mythology, saying:

> "Now he goes,
> With no less presence, but with much more love,
> Than young Alcides, when he did redeem
> The virgin tribute paid by howling Troy
> To the sea monster. I stand for sacrifice;
> The rest aloof are the Dardanian wives..." (III.ii.53-58)

The image of a young maiden being sacrificed to a sea monster is a powerful illustration for the risk that Portia will be married to a man who does not appreciate her true worth, but is captivated only by the promise of wealth that accompanies marriage to her. Although she is the primary sufferer, it is not just her own personal happiness that is at stake. Rather she sees herself as a participant in the larger struggle to maintain a higher currency for human relationships than money, and to form a marriage contract that will be more than an exchange of goods. (Another interesting dynamic of this classical reference is that it parallels later events of the play: Hesione's sacrifice to the monster is a harsh punishment exacted because of a breach in contract, and Portia will later appear as a Hercules herself and redeem her husband.)

Completing one of several tripartite structures within the play, Shakespeare reiterates the theme of contract after Bassanio has chosen the casket containing Portia's portrait. The primary contract of the play, the "merry bargain" struck by Antonio and Shylock in Act I was initially for purely economic purposes, and leads in Act IV to a desperate dispute over the value of human life. The second iteration of contracts occurs when Morocco must swear according to the wishes of Portia's father. (Interestingly, his answer is a thoroughly ambiguous "Nor will not" (II.i.43), suggesting that he has attempted to dodge the terms of the contract.) This is a suitor's oath, and like the oaths of many wooing lovers throughout Shakespeare's plays, contains a mix of the altruistic and the selfish.

But at Portia's pledge of marriage to Bassanio, we see a higher form of the same theme - she establishes a new contract, which involves an exchange of goods, but operates on a currency of faithfulness:

> But now I was the lord
> Of this fair mansion, master of my servants,
> Queen o'er myself; and even now, but now,
> This house, these servants and this same myself
> Are yours, my lord's. I give them with this ring,
> Which when you part from, lose, or give away,
> Let it presage the ruin of your love
> And be my vantage to exclaim on you (III.ii.167-174).

The outside world soon presents a threat to her newly achieved comedic ending, when Antonio's letter arrives. Portia does not accept these circumstances passively, but instead ventures from Belmont, seeking to surreptitiously uphold her harmonic vision, actively crafting a harmonious denouement. Portia's steps forth as high-minded comic artisan. She steps into Venice, a materialistic, male-dominated realm, and into the court of justice, where Antonio's life is being treated with an impartiality far removed from the idealism of the world of Belmont.

In a sense then Portia, or a Portia, is dramatically expected before her arrival at the courtroom. The Duke's address to Shylock at the beginning of the trial scene draws a connection between the court room and the theater, showing that the audience has come to watch the trial expecting to enjoy the satisfaction of a comedic narrative structure.

> Make room, and let him stand before our face.
> Shylock, the world thinks, and I think so too,
> That thou but leadest this fashion of thy malice
> To the last hour of act; and then 'tis thought
> Thou'lt show thy mercy and remorse more strange
> Than is thy strange apparent cruelty... (IV.i.16-19).

The duke emphasizes the plurality of the audience, and clears the way, so that Shylock seems to be standing center-stage. By emphasizing the inner thoughts and expectations of the audience, which he calls "the world" (IV.i.17) he suggests that this desire is universal. Furthermore, the audience views Shylock as an actor, a comic villain who at the end of the play will suddenly remove his mask of cruelty and show mercy, thereby confirming their trust in a universal order of justice in the world. There is a meta-theatrical element to the court scene then, which mimics the experience of watching a play. The audience, according to the Duke, also expects that Shylock will be "touched with human gentleness and love" (IV.i.25), that Shylock will affirm their belief in a common human compassion and kindness. The audience longs to see a comedy, and does not want to see the villain win. To conclude, he posits coldly, "We all expect a gentle answer Jew" (IV.i.33), emphasizing that Shylock appears to the audience not as an individual but as a category; he is a villain who is bound to play a certain role that will uphold the values of the audience.

But Portia does more than attempt to satisfy the audience's desire for affirmation of their values. Nor does she gratify Gratiano's savage demands for vengeance. Instead, she seeks to teach. Hapgood especially emphasizes her educational efforts in the courtroom: "Undoubtedly, Portia's methods in the trial scene (as elsewhere) are highhanded. Yet they seem to me to be defensible, not as those of a judge administering the law but as those of a teacher presenting a series of lessons in it" (Hapgood. *The Gentle Bond*, 21). Portia uses the courtroom as a forum to educate the citizens, and especially Shylock, in the highest values of mercy and compassion, and in the limitations of the strict enforcement of contract as a means to bring about justice. Portia's famous speech on mercy is eloquent and persuasive, but proves ineffective in swaying Shylock from his course. It is actually quite puzzling that she attempts to persuade Shylock with an appeal to a Christian understanding of justice and salvation, saying, "Though justice be thy plea, consider this:/That in the course of justice, none of us/ Should see salvation" (IV.i.197-199) If she knows anything about the basic differences between Jewish and Christian understandings of the afterlife, then she cannot possibly mean to persuade Shylock with this argument. Her speech is rather directed towards the predominately Christian audience, to teach them what it is they are to expect from Shylock.

By further stoking Shylock's rage with what is perhaps a deliberately obnoxious argument, she also sets him up to experience an even more shocking dramatic reversal later on, taking a playwright's role in crafting the outcome of the trial. Leggatt, in explaining Portia's strategy: "As Bassanio entered and understood the conventions of Belmont, Portia has now entered and understood the special conventions of Shylock's mind, the diabolical game of "justice." And she destroys Shylock with the weapon most fatal to convention –parody" (Leggatt, Alexander. *Shakespeare's Comedy of Love.* 144.). However, Portia is not only teaching us, the audience, about the nature of justice when taken to its extreme. She is also, at the dramatic level, attempting to instruct the onlookers and participants in the room by means of comedy, albeit a dark one, showing the absurdity of Shylock's demand for literalism, and the importance of mercy.

Portia's attempt at educating her onlookers is then put to the test, for she tells Shylock to "beg mercy of the Duke"

(IV.i.362), and even gives Antonio sway over the outcome of the trial, asking, "What mercy can you render him, Antonio?" (IV.i.177). In addition to making clear to Shylock his reliance on the mercy of others, she also testing whether or not her attempt at educating the public has been successful. This is legally dubious, for while the Duke certainly wields authority in the case, it is certainly questionable whether Antonio should be making these decisions. It is also a risky decision on her part regarding the life of Shylock, for the "mercy" which Antonio renders him is also of a dubious nature. It is in large part the ruthless penalty exacted from Shylock that has made it increasingly difficult for modern readers to regard this play as simply a comedy. Bryant argues that Antonio's demand that Shylock bequeath his whole estate to Lorenzo and Jessica (IV.i.387-389) is unacceptable if we accept that Shylock is a character with any depth: "...the last three [lines] give approval to an abduction which can be approved only if Shylock is totally villainous or if he is simply a stereotype of the despicable miser of New Comedy." (Bryant Jr., J.A. *Shakespeare & the Uses of Comedy.* 91) When examined from this perspective, Portia's decision to put Shylock at the mercy of Antonio seems somewhat reckless, or to result from naive idealism.

It may also be posited that in utilizing a satirical approach to counter Shylock's irrationality she is risking the perpetuation of the very problem he represents. When Bassanio encourages her to bend the law to Antonio's favor, she responds with the firm conviction that:

> It must not be...
> 'Twill be recorded for a precedent,
> And many an error by the same example
> Will rush into the state. It cannot be (IV.i.217-221).

If her logic is taken seriously, then her strategy for defeating Shylock is through absurd literalism, which is poetically effective but legally quite dangerous. The resolution that Portia achieves is by this measure an imperfect one - by the end of the play, we appear to, but have not entirely moved beyond the problems of Shylock's primitive contractual understanding of justice, and we have not truly reconciled the effects of his irrationality to the demands of a larger moral order.

Appropriately, the audience of the play itself is invited in Act V to consider the nature of harmony, and to compare the harmony that Portia achieves against the realm of the ideal. This comparison is first encouraged by the discussion of Jessica and Lorenzo, who have a poignant and playful exchange centered on tragic love stories from the classical tradition. Then, to the backdrop of music emanating from Portia's house, Lorenzo conjures up strong Neoplatonic imagery, sadly comparing the discrepancy between the harmony of the spheres and the imperfection and decay of life on Earth.

> Sit, Jessica. Look how the floor of heaven
> Is thick inlaid with patens of bright gold.
> There's not the smallest orb which thou behold'st

But in his motion like an angel sings,
Still quiring to the young-eyed cherubins;
Such harmony is in immortal souls,
But whilst this muddy vesture of decay
Doth grossly close it in, we cannot hear it (V.i.58-65).

This brief lecture makes explicit the Neoplatonic imagery that underlies the complex blend of tragic and comic themes throughout the play. Lorenzo's description of the golden heavens is also reminiscent of the gold imagery frequently associated with Portia, who has spent much of the play struggling to construct a pleasing harmony from the discord of the Venetian world. Leggatt elucidates this passage beautifully, touching on both its humor and poignancy: "When comedy measures itself against tragedy it can mock it easily enough, for its own vision is essentially different. But beyond tragedy is the vision of permanent, immutable harmony-- a vision that is closer to comedy's own concerns; and here there is a deeper sadness in measuring the distance between two imperfect human lovers and the principle of love that orders the universe" (Leggatt 149). Comedy and tragedy share a concern with the deeper harmony and patterns underlying human life, and both explore the possibility of reconciliation of reality to an underlying sense of the ideal. Shakespeare therefore invites us to consider that, in participating in the activity of theater, we are inquiring into the nature and possibility of the ideal in the world.

Portia is then led to consider, as she reenters the realm of the worldly ideal at Belmont, where she learned the high aristocratic values that she attempted to take with her into Venice, whether or not she has succeeded in her attempt to bring about something resembling a cosmic harmony. Portia here has a realization: she says, "Nothing is good, I see, without respect;/ Methinks it sounds much sweeter than by day" (V.i.99-100). This conversation with Nerissa reflects her realization that the beauty of music is a relative beauty, derived from its surroundings. This insight is momentous in light of Portia's ongoing effort to harmonize her reality. She goes on to call her own voice a bad one, saying "He knows me as the blind man knows the cuckoo, / By the bad voice" (V.i.112-113). If this statement can be taken as a reference to her own efforts throughout the play, it suggests that Portia is acknowledging the imperfect nature of the resolution that she has affected. Portia sees in the garden that she cannot bring about an absolute, Neoplatonic good, but that she can affect a relative good, a provisional harmony.

In this way the play can be understood as a comedy that struggles to come to terms with an often un-comedic world. Recalling the initial distinction drawn between Antonio's tragic resignation and Portia's determination for comic negotiation, we witness a larger thematic movement, with the effort to actively construct a comedic reality emerging as a partial answer to the problems created by tragedy. The provisional harmony the audience receives at the end of the play does not sufficiently address the injustice underlying mercantile societies, nor resolve all the tensions in the characters' relationships to one another. In accepting this imperfect ending, however, we can better grasp what

Bryant describes as "that principle which unites Shakespeare's comedies with his tragedies: the principle whereby we are urged to accept substitutes until a true king be by, to take things as they come to us, at face value whenever that is possible but always as a gift deserving of our respect and our effort at understanding" (Bryant, 95).

The beauty of the ending of this play is that it is emblematic of the ongoing human struggle to create new, meaningful realities out of the conflicts that assail us, sculpting harmonious images from the gray stuff of the given world. This struggle is represented by the activity of comedy, which through its apparently anarchic course allows an audience to witness the construction of a new and pleasing reality in the imagination. Shakespeare's complex comedy comments on this process, while Portia simultaneously accomplishes the creation of her own comedy before us. Whether the patterns of harmony and beauty we model our hopes for resolution after have true existence anywhere in nature or the heavens, or whether they are creations of the mind, products of infinite longing and skillful artifice -this, however, remains mysterious.

Works Cited

Shakespeare, William. Ed. Kenneth Myrick. The Signet Classic Shakespeare: *The Merchant of Venice.* New York: Penguin, 1998.

Leggatt, Alexander. "The Fourth and Fifth Acts." *Shakespeare's Comedy of Love.* The Signet Classic Shakespeare: *The Merchant of Venice.* New York: Penguin, 1998.

Hapgood, Robert. "Portia And The Merchant Of Venice: The Gentle Bond."*Modern Language Quarterly* 28.1 (1967): 19. *Academic Search Premier.* Web. 16 May 2012.

Bryant Jr., J.A. "The Merchant of Venice." *The Uses of Comedy.* Lexington: The University Press of Kentucky, 1986.

On the Rights of Men and Women: The Second Presidential Debate

Demetri Vincze

Women across the United States face one crippling obstacle in the workplace: not being able to make it home in time to make dinner. Unlike his opponent, Mitt Romney noted this critical problem in the second presidential debate. While Barack Hussein Obama and his liberal cronies have identified unequal pay for women not only as a gender discrimination issue, but as a "family issue" and a "middle-class issue," my fellow staunch conservatives and I have resisted this capitulation to the feminist agenda and worked to protect a woman's right to make dinner. Leftist radicals such as Obama claim that feminism is about treating women the same as men—"equal rights"—but we know better. As our patron saint Pat Robertson once said, "(T)he feminist agenda is not about equal rights for women. It is about a socialist, anti-family political movement that encourages women to leave their husbands, kill their children, practice witchcraft, destroy capitalism and become lesbians." Instead of stemming the tide against this anti-American movement, Obama's failure of leadership has been again made manifest in his signing of the Lilly Ledbetter Fair Pay Act of 2009.

Radicals, who often find occupation in the field of Social Work, like to look at the world through a paradigm of critical analysis. This view suggests that there are implicit and explicit aims of policy, sometimes influenced by power relations between various groups. Though this paradigm is foreign to my fellow conservatives, who often believe in the literal interpretation of things, I will attempt to apply it to the Lilly Ledbetter Fair Pay Act (LLFPA).

Most Americans support women's rights because Obama has created a culture of dependency. At least forty-seven percent of Americans are entitled leaches that are 'takers-more-than-makers.' In other words, they now embody typical female characteristics. The Democratic Party, infiltrated by the feminist elite, has taken advantage of this window of opportunity to convince women, and some weak-minded men, that there should be equal rights in America. Only by these pathetic and extreme measures have the Democrats been able to scrounge up enough support to pass the LLFPA. But strong, independent-minded conservatives, unbiased by the 'lamestream' media understand the true context behind the passage of this act.

White men have long been discriminated against in the United States. The fact that we outnumber our lesser female counterparts overwhelmingly in both chambers of Congress, in the halls of the Supreme Court, and in the government generally is inconsequential. The last century or so has been marked by the creation of special rights for women: suffrage, access to birth control, and innumerable others. This regression, at the expense of dinner preparation and other wifely duties, is an unacceptable violation of men's rights. The (LLFPA) only continues this troubling trend. Not only is this a power struggle between men and women, it is a battle between the government and the corporation. By mandating equal pay for women, big government is destroying business. What only we conservatives can see is that by regulating equal pay, the government is only getting in the way of the private sector's more efficient provision of equal pay. Government is not the solution, it is the problem. Pro-government ideologues think that the government has to step in to protect the worker from the corporation. But one has to look only as far as the distribution of income between CEOs and their workers to witness that a corporation distributes to each what he deserves.

Despite the noble resistance of conservatives and corporations, the ill-effects of the LLFPA are beginning to be felt by the American people. By amending the statutory definition of "unlawful employment practice" to help women to challenge inequities in pay under Title VII of the Civil Rights Act, the law makes pay discrimination a greater liability for corporations. It tells women that they are entitled to receiving back pay to compensate for discrepancies, even though their work is inherently inferior. Moreover the law is made effective as of May 28th, 2007. Thus the most important of American people, the corporation, is heavily impacted by this development. However, I am confident that corporations will find a way around this legislation. In *Ledbetter v. Goodyear Tire & Rubber Co., 550 U.S. 618 (2007)*, Lilly Ledbetter was denied her claim to equal pay because she did not report the violation of her "rights" within 300 days of their infringement. Luckily, the LLFPA does nothing to change this time restriction. Corporations will still be able to constitutionally pay men more than women, as they did in the *Ledbetter* case, uninhibited by the iron fist of Obama's communist government. Justice is served: unequal pay for unequal work.

Despite this latest nominal setback in the fight for men's rights, I am confident that men will come together to overcome this challenge. Discrimination against white men, masked in another form as "affirmative action," is beginning to erode. The Supreme Court will soon rule against these discriminatory policies, providing a ray of hope to those who love America—the conservatives. If we can fix our mistakes on one front, we can fix them on another. Even though the LLFPA is mostly symbolic in its protection of women's rights, an even-clearer message must be sent to American women: the Constitution entitles you to no special rights. The election of Mitt Romney will usher in a long-overdue period in which men are no longer unduly discriminated against. Because of his belief in America and protection of traditional gender roles, Mitt Romney will repeal and replace the Lilly Ledbetter Fair Pay Act of 2009 on day one of his presidency. With what he will replace it remains unclear—we'll have to wait until January 20th to see—but hopefully it will act to rectify the numerous past injustices against white men.

In the Shadow of Portia:
Jessica's Unsuccessful Navigation between Patriarchy and Matriarchy in *The Merchant of Venice*

Emily E. Oleson

Much has been written about the figure of Portia in Shakespeare's *The Merchant of Venice*; she is often venerated as one of Shakespeare's most thoroughly (and unexpectedly) liberated women. Much less has been written, however, about Jessica, who also enacts her liberation in interesting ways in the course of the play. Both Portia and Jessica begin the play under the control of their overbearing fathers; their actions throughout the play represent a response to this patriarchal power, a response that consists largely of rejection. Portia, as a true comic character, nimbly navigates within a patriarchal world, simultaneously following its rules and asserting her own dominance. By contrast, Jessica takes more radical action but experiences less success. Jessica expresses ambiguities and uncertainties as an active woman in a patriarchal society, as well as subtly communicating a deep concern about her own identity and worth.

To understand Jessica's complexity, one must first examine the role of Portia and the significance of Belmont, her home. Belmont acts as the comic "green space" of the play, symbolizing an idealized world that escapes the economic and political realities of Venice. It is within this sphere that Portia's influence operates, and while Belmont never wholly intersects with Venice, Portia is able to bring some of Belmont's idealism into Venice through her actions as Balthasar. The idealism of Belmont and Portia's ability to bring this near-utopia partly into Venice exemplify Portia's ascendency as a character, not just to critics but also to others in the play. Portia shows herself to be the paragon of female power, able to navigate any situation and to earn the deference of all those around her.

Even prior to her triumph in the courtroom, Portia wins the respect of the audience and Bassanio through the casket trial in Act 3, Scene 2. While explicitly respecting the rules her father's will set out for her, Portia manipulates the stipulations of the casket test to achieve her desired goals, displaying for the first time her ability to overcome masculine power structures. Critic Robert Hapgood finds "in Portia's lines to Bassanio (before he chooses) a host of subliminal suggestions, of the sort by which a skillful teacher leads a responsive student to make his own 'discoveries'" (25). Thus, Portia proves her authority not only over her father's will but also over Bassanio; in the first case, she holds the power of revision, and in the second she holds the power of teaching. With the giving of her ring, Portia seems to give Bassanio the power, even saying, "This house, these servants, and this same myself/ Are yours, my lord's" (3.2.170-171). However, Bassanio continuously defers to Portia throughout this scene. Before following the scroll's direction to kiss Portia, he asks her leave; even then, he is uncertain of his triumph "Until confirmed, signed, ratified by" Portia (3.2.139, 148). On the entrance of his friends from Venice, Bassanio even asks Portia's permission to bid them welcome, acknowledging Portia's continued ownership and control of Belmont (3.2.221-224). Portia has already claimed the power in her relationship with Bassanio and in doing so has convinced the audience of her tremendous competence.

Portia's reappearance as Balthasar in Act 4 raises her above every other character in the play as the only figure capable of restoring equity and order. Just as she navigates between her father's will and her own desires in the casket test, she now navigates between justice and mercy. Faced with Shylock's legal but clearly unjust insistence on taking Antonio's flesh, Portia's "remedy is equity – not simply justice or simply mercy, but justice tempered by mercy" (Hapgood 20). Another opposition Portia navigates through in this scene is that of masculine and feminine; she is able to present herself as a man without being questioned by the men of the court. Portia's disguise as Balthasar allows her to be simultaneously masculine and feminine, simultaneously a lawyer and an heiress. Like many of Shakespeare's comic heroines, Portia "simply activates the masculine resources within the normal feminine personality without negating her essential femininity" (Berggren 20). Dusinberre further points out that Portia's disguise does not obscure her character so much as it allows her to express her "poise and control of the male world;" after all, Portia in her identity as a lady "is always something of a lawyer" (267-268). Thus, Portia maneuvers successfully between two seemingly contrasting identities as well as between the philosophical ideals of the trial. In the process, she displays her insight, intelligence, and flexibility, reinforcing the audience's perceptions of her as an ideal woman. Much more could be said about Portia's character, particularly with regard to the ring trick of Act 5, but for the purposes of this paper, further discussion here is unnecessary.

Portia's power represents a feminism founded upon the strength and insight of a woman in the green space of Belmont; Jessica's feminism carries a different strength, a more troubled insight, and a Venetian realism still present in Jessica's Belmont scenes. Nevertheless, Jessica demonstrates a belief in her own agency through both her words and her actions.

In her first scene of the play (Act 2, Scene 3), Jessica reveals her unhappiness in her father's home, as well as her plans to rectify the situation. Having lamented her hatred for her father's religion and way of life, Jessica exclaims, "O Lorenzo, / If thou keep promise, I shall end this strife, /Become a Christian and thy loving wife!" (2.3.16-21). While Lorenzo is given one action ("keep promise"), Jessica assigns three actions to herself: she will "end this strife," "become a Christian," and become Lorenzo's wife. Though necessary, Lorenzo is not a knight in shining armor with the power to ride in and rescue Jessica; instead, Lorenzo is a condition for Jessica's own action toward an escape. Jessica's language also points to her desire to redefine herself; rather than seeing herself as a Jew and as Shylock's daughter, she proposes a new definition as a Christian and Lorenzo's wife.

Jessica's active phrasing is followed through to its natural conclusion in her elopement. Unlike Portia, who maneuvers within the boundaries of her father's will, Jessica escapes entirely from her father's will by eloping with Lorenzo. Hapgood claims that the contrast between Jessica and Portia "serves to distinguish Portia's poetic license from Jessica's simple license. Jessica *defies* her father's will and, as Burckhardt finely observes (p. 253), literally throws her father's casket to Lorenzo" (31). Here we see both the play and the literature discuss Jessica's elopement and find themselves once again experimenting with caskets. Sigmund Freud's reading of the casket scenes emphasizes symbolism, saying that "caskets are also women, symbols of what is essential in woman" and that Portia's leaden casket represents the goddess of death (292). This is, perhaps, too distant a symbolism to be applied here; instead, the caskets might represent the limits and restrictions placed on Portia and Jessica. Portia's image, after all, is placed within the confines of the casket. Interestingly, Portia is let out of her casket directly by Bassanio; after this, she is able to move freely through the spaces of the play, even emerging into the political space of Venice. By contrast, Jessica leaves Shylock's house (her own casket) largely by her own volition; Lorenzo provides the necessary condition, but he waits passively while Jessica collects her things and steps out of the house. Having freed herself, though, Jessica never experiences the same degree of agency and mobility possessed by Portia, undercutting the feminism of the play by suggesting that the freest woman is fundamentally dependent on a man for her freedom and competence.

To further complicate the casket question in Jessica's case, we have an additional casket – the casket full of her father's wealth. In her dialogue from the window with Lorenzo, Jessica says, "Here, catch this casket; it is worth the pains" (2.6.33). This simple line elucidates two significant aspects of Jessica's feminism: her relationship to her future husband and her relationship to her father. The first half of the line is a direct command; Jessica takes power in her relationship with Lorenzo by commanding that he catch the casket, adding not so much as a "please you." Jessica does not fall into the gender role of quiet, subservient wife, but instead exercises verbal control over her lover. However, the taking of the casket is a more ambiguous image. As quoted in Hapgood, Burckhardt uses the theft of the casket to describe Jessica and Lorenzo's relationship as "lawless, financed by theft and engineered through a gross breach of trust" (31). This reading sees the theft simply as an indication of the law breaking associated with a daughter denying her father's will. However, the casket holds deeper clues to an understanding of Jessica's condition. When choosing those things to take with her, Jessica seems to think only of wealth as contained in the casket. The concern with wealth demonstrates that, however unsettled Jessica is by her father's identity and economic practices, she cannot escape the importance of money, not only to her father but also to her society. Furthermore, in taking the casket with her into her future life, she brings along the emblem of her restriction as a woman.

Thus, her "Catch this casket" line highlights both the extent and the limitations of Jessica's feminism.

The doublespeak of "Catch this casket" moves the reader toward the struggles and ambiguities inherent in Jessica's movement toward freedom. Throughout the play, Jessica references feelings of shame, which point to an understanding of her psychology as conflicted and self-denigrating.

Jessica's first mention of shame in the play displays a conflict between her Jewish identity and her desired Christian one. In her first scene of the play, Jessica is already preoccupied with the experience of shame:

> Alack, what heinous sin is it in me
> To be ashamed to be my father's child!
> But though I am a daughter to his blood,
> I am not to his manners. O Lorenzo,
> If thou keep promise, I shall end this strife,
> Become a Christian and thy loving wife! (2.3.16-21).

While some readings might suggest that Jessica feels it is sinful to be ashamed of her Judaism, another reading suggests an almost-punning response to Launcelot's lines a moment before. Launcelot famously puns, "if a Christian do not play the knave and get thee, I am much deceived," simultaneously implying that a Christian (Lorenzo) will get her in marriage and that a Christian illegitimately *begot* her (2.3.11-13). With this remark in mind, Jessica's exclamation ironically responds that, instead of being ashamed to be illegitimate, she is ashamed of her legitimacy. By extension, she is more ashamed of her Jewish blood than she would be by the thought of adultery; by labeling this a "heinous sin," Jessica aligns herself with Shakespeare's many Christian characters that speak of adultery and incest in an almost phobic manner, considering them worse than any other moral indecency of the plays. In spite of the irony, though, it is clear that Jessica genuinely experiences her conflict as one of shame. She is both ashamed of her Jewish identity and ashamed of her desire to escape it. And while this early passage suggests the possibility to "end this strife," Jessica continues to show herself ashamed.

Even in the scene of Jessica's active escape from Shylock's house, her dialogue is plagued by the idea of shame. This time, the shame stems less from her Jewish identity and more from her "exchange" of clothing, gender, and religious identity:

> Jessica: Here, catch this casket; it is worth the pains.
> I am glad 'tis night, you do not look on me,
> For I am much ashamed of my exchange.
> But love is blind and lovers cannot see
> The pretty follies that themselves commit;
> For if they could, Cupid himself would blush
> To see me thus transformed to a boy.
> Lorenzo: Descend, for you must be my torchbearer.
> Jessica: What, must I hold a candle to my shames?
> (2.6.33-41).

In this case, Jessica associates shame with her desire not to be seen ("you do not look on me"), which she connects with the rhetoric of blind love. This reveals anxieties both about the possibility of Lorenzo's love for her and about her new identity as Lorenzo's wife.

Her gladness that the darkness will not allow Lorenzo to see her in her boy's clothes suggests her doubt about Lorenzo's love. She seems to wonder if her disguise will remove from her the only piece of her identity that Lorenzo could (in her mind) love – her sexuality. Stripped of her religious and ethnic identity by her exit from her father's house, Jessica fears that the removal of her sexual identity will reduce her to nothing until such a time as she can don her new religious and ethnic identity. Jessica worries that in the meantime, her lack of clear identity will cause Lorenzo to abandon her, leaving her permanently without her new Christian-gentile identity. This anxiety shows the degree to which Jessica feels her identity as impermanent and dependent upon external conditions rather than internal character. And even if Lorenzo's love can bring her safely into her new identity, Jessica expresses feelings of shame even toward the ideas of love and wifehood. She suggests that love must be blind or "Cupid himself would blush" at the follies of lovers (2.6.38). This implies that love inherently leads to folly and is therefore shameful. Even her new identity as Lorenzo's lover and wife – chosen as a means to escape the shame of her father's Jewish heritage – calls up in her a response of shame. Thus, every aspect of her fluid identity, every "exchange" occurring in Act 2, Scene 6, becomes a source of shame for Jessica.

Further elaborating on her anxiety of identity, Jessica continually defines herself with respect to other characters in the play, beginning with her father and Lorenzo. Even in some of her most self-affirming passages, Jessica defines herself by her relationships to the men.

> But though I am a daughter to his blood,
> I am not to his manners. O Lorenzo,
> If thou keep promise, I shall end this strife,
> Become a Christian and thy loving wife! (2.3.18-21).

She firsts dissociates her identity from her father's blood, then remakes her self-definition by announcing that she will become Lorenzo's "loving wife." Instead of making her own identity with regard to her own beliefs and thoughts (as some of Shakespeare's tragic men do), Jessica remakes her identity around her husband-to-be. In addition, she twice frames her escape from the old identity as conditional on things she has no control over. In the above quote, the condition is "If thou [Lorenzo] keep promise;" in her next scene, the condition becomes "if my fortune be not crost" (2.3.20, 2.5.55). Though it is clear that Jessica sees herself as an agent in her life and identity, she nevertheless demonstrates doubt and dependence in these conditional statements.

Even after Jessica has redefined her religion and ethnicity through her marriage, she continues to define herself in terms of others, particularly in what Adelman calls her "absurdly self-denigrating paean to heavenly Portia" (9). To Lorenzo's question about her opinion of Portia, Jessica replies:

> Past all expressing....
> Why, if two gods should play some heavenly match
> And on the wager lay two earthly women,
> And Portia one, there must be something else
> Pawned with the other, for the poor rude world

Hath not her fellow (3.5.72,78-82).

This comparative self-definition is perhaps the most destructive of all. Rather than merely limiting her identity to her relationships with men, this understanding of self is laden with feelings of despondent inadequacy. Portia's ascendency – her perceived moral uprightness, her beauty, her wealth, and her undeniable power – leave Jessica feeling "poor", "rude," and unvalued.

Shakespeare uses humor and comedy to relieve the tensions within the play, and his treatment of the various tensions raised by Jessica is no different. Parten argues that the ring episode serves to re-establish sexual order in the primary plot; in a similar way, Jessica and Lorenzo's dialogue at the opening of Act 5, Scene 1 re-establishes sexual order between the play's secondary active woman and her husband. They lightheartedly compare the night of the scene to nights in the stories of famous betrayed lovers – Troilus, Thisbe, Dido, and Medea. Then they move closer to home:

Lorenzo: In such a night
          Did Jessica steal from the wealthy Jew,
          And with an unthrift love did run from Venice
          As far as Belmont.
Jessica: In such a night
          Did young Lorenzo swear he loved her well,
          Stealing her soul with many vows of faith,
          And ne'er a true one (5.1.14-19).

The staggered sharing of the lines indicates to the audience the lovers' union; even as they joke about unfaithfulness, their poetic unity dismisses any concerns about their future fidelity. However, the lines also conclude a preoccupation with theft that has run through the play since Act 2, Scene 6 when Lorenzo says "When you shall please to play the thieves for wives" (2.6.23). Lorenzo now paints Jessica as having stolen from her father, both in the sense of running away and in the sense of theft. Jessica escalates the comic argument by accusing Lorenzo of stealing her soul, ironically reinterpreting her sought-after conversion as forcible theft by Lorenzo.

Under all of this banter about infidelity and robbery lies a mutual anxiety of abandonment. While Lorenzo may fear that Jessica could run away again, Jessica's suggestion that Lorenzo could steal her soul represents a greater problem. Perhaps if Lorenzo were to abandon Jessica, he would take her newly saved soul along with him. Lorenzo's reply that Jessica did "slander her love" serves to keep this anxiety at bay, at least for the audience (5.1.22). However, Jessica is silenced by an approaching messenger, and the audience does not learn whether Lorenzo's assurances have assuaged her anxiety.

Jessica's final words give insight into her state of melancholy, which is at once particular and universal. Lorenzo gives a beautiful monologue about the beauty of the night and of music, threading the word "sweet" throughout. He calls Jessica "sweet soul," he refers to the "sweet" moonlight, he calls music "sweet harmony," and he declares that "such harmony is in immortal souls," bringing the audience back to Jessica's sweet soul

(5.1.49,54,57,63). In this way, Lorenzo frames Jessica's soul, the moonlight, and music as beautiful in similar ways; all to him bear a "sweet harmony." But Jessica does not feel the harmony in her soul so clearly; she feels instead the melancholy dissonance of music: "I am never merry when I hear sweet music" (5.1.69). Lorenzo explains this away by speaking of music's ability to make frolicking animals stop in their tracks; he ignores the very personal nature of Jessica's statement to discuss the melancholy universally conjured up by music. Jessica, though, may be specifically feeling the dissonance caused by her anxieties and her confused identity as accentuated by the contrastingly harmonized music. But this tragic voice cannot persist in comedy, and so Jessica fades into silence for the remainder of the play. We are left with Lorenzo's generalizations about the power of music, without Jessica's intimate relationship to that power. Jessica's final line hints at her lack of happiness in spite of the restored harmony of comedy. For everyone else at Belmont, the harmonized ending will be a cause of joy, but for Jessica, it will be a melancholic reminder of her still-disunited self.

Though Portia is able to bring about a comic ending for most of the characters in the play, her success adds to the tragedy Jessica experiences. Jessica can neither rise above the patriarchal influences in her life nor match the magic of the matriarch. Though she exits the play with a happy and reasonably equitable marriage, freedom from the direct influence of her father, and the hope that she has been successfully Christianized, Jessica nevertheless ends with a fragmented, obscured, and worthless vision of herself. Thus the "sweet music" of comedy is hung about with the blindness and melancholy of tragedy, so that we must end the play saying with Jessica that we are never merry when we hear sweet music.

Works Cited

Adelman, Janet. "Her Father's Blood: Race, Conversion, and Nation in The Merchant of Venice." *Representations*, 81.1. University of California Press (2003).

Berggren, Paula S. "The Woman's Part: Female Sexuality as Power in Shakespeare's Plays." *The Woman's Part: Feminist Criticism of Shakespeare*, Carolyn Ruth Swift Lenz, Gayle Greene, and Carol Thomas Neely, ed. Chicago: University of Illinois Press, 1980.

Dusinberre, Juliet. *Shakespeare and the Nature of Women*. New York: Harper and Rowe Publishers, Inc., 1975.

Freud, Siegmund. *The Theme of the Three Caskets*. Accessed via www.ebookbrowse.com. Web.

Hapgood, Robert. "Portia and the Merchant of Venice." *Modern Language Quarterly* 28 (1967): 19-32.

Parten, Anne. "Re-establishing Sexual Order: the Ring Episode in *The Merchant of Venice*." *Women's Studies* 9(2) (1982): 145-156.

Shakespeare, William. *The Merchant of Venice*. Kenneth Myrick, ed. New York: Signet Classic, 1998.

Two Ways to Call upon the Gods

Cami Christopulos

The parados of a play is not the opening lines, yet its importance exists as it introduces the background information and the chorus, whom will be seen throughout the entire play. In the parados in *Oedipus the King*, written by Greek tragedian Sophocles, the chorus describes that their city of Thebes is being destroyed by a plague. People in their city are dying, and the land and women suffering. They call upon various gods to help them end this disastrous time. The desperate chorus is illustrated in both the translations of David Grene (lines 151-215) and Robert Fagles (lines 168-244). Although similar in content, the contrasts between the two are numerous in terms of how the chorus uses poetic and rhetorical devices to describe situations and deities.

The chorus of the play helps set the tone in the parados, which is evident in *Oedipus the King*. However, the two translations of the chorus's tone vary in the chorus's speech. From lines 151-167, Grene presents the chorus as being fearful as they state "terror and trembling hold my heart" (153-154). Grene also portrays them as perplexed, described by the strophe and antistrophe by uneasiness through their movement. In contrast, Fagles begins to illustrate the chorus's anger in a stage direction stating that they "*march around the altar, chanting.*" By presenting the chorus not only as angry but as perplexed through their constant rhetorical questioning, Fagles portrays the chorus to be a more active and aggressive group than is portrayed in Grene's translation. The tone shifts for both translations, lines 168-189 in Grene's and lines 190-258 in Fagles's, when the chorus begins to describe what has occurred in Thebes concerning the plague, as they become more melancholy and angry about the plague destroying their city. These tones are illustrated through the drawn out sentences, only continuing through various forms of punctuation, and the continuous referral to death. Similarly, the tone shifts again for both until the end as the chorus is more forceful, demanding revival of their people and city by calling on the gods. Fagles presents this shift by the chorus's exclamations to various gods from lines 228-244: "Artemis, Huntress, torches flaring over the eastern ridges-ride Death down in pain!" (235-237). On the contrary, Grene illustrates the shift through constant referral to Apollo, "Lycean King, I beg to be at our side for help" (205). Through careful diction and syntax choices, both translators are able to convey the chorus as worried, confused, and determined all at once.

In tragedian plays, the chorus is meant to fulfill many purposes. In this parados, the chorus reveals details of the present situation. Throughout much of the middle section, lines 168-189 in Grene's and 190-258 in Fagles's, there is constant repetition of the words "no" and "death". These words portray a negative connotation, which helps illustrate the chorus's anger toward the situation. Grene describes "no growing children," "no women bearing the pangs of childbirth," and due to the "unnumbered deaths of its people the city dies" (171, 172, 177-178). Similarly, Fagles has the chorus portray that there is "no end," with "numberless deaths on deaths" and states Thebes as the "city of death" (191, 204, 211). Although the chorus presents their worries in similar content in both translations, the actual context of each can be viewed differently, specifically when the chorus talks about death approaching the mothers and wives. In Grene's translation, the chorus states "grey-haired mothers and wives everywhere stand at the altar's edge, suppliant, moaning; the hymn to the healing God rings out but with it the wailing voices are blended" (181-187). In these lines, Grene portrays the women to be suffering through the word "moaning," yet the statement is not powerful or descriptive of the women, which Fagles presents in his translation: "the young wives and gray-haired mothers with them cling to the altars, trailing in from all over the city...the suffering rises wails for mercy rise and the wild hymn for the Healer blazes out clashing with our sobs our cries of morning" (209-210, 212-215). Through this translation, the chorus details the action of the women as they "cling to the altars" and the hymn "blazes out." Through careful choice of diction, the translators allow the chorus to portray the current events of Thebes in different ways.

In comparing how the chorus praises the gods in both translations, not only are the structures of their speeches different, but also their emphasis on the praise of various deities to help them save the city of Thebes. The chorus in Grene's translation mainly focuses on Apollo. For example, in the beginning of their

147

speech, they call to Apollo to help them clear up their confusion. They also call on Athene and Artemis, but do not speak much of them. From lines 197-215, the chorus calls to Zeus, Apollo, and Dionysus to save them from the plague because of their specialties, as they refer to Apollo as "Lycean King" and Dionysus as "Bacchic God", showing their respect for each. Dissimilarly, Fagles does not have the chorus focus on one god for a specific amount of time. In the beginning of the parados, they cry to Zeus and Apollo to explain what is happening to their city, and also call to Athena and Artemis to help them. In the end of the speech, the chorus calls to the gods one at a time, first Zeus, then Apollo, then Artemis, and finally Dionysus, praising them for their specialties that could aid them in ending the plague. Through this method, Fagles illustrates that the chorus is not relying on one god to help them, but rather many at once, in contrast to Grene as the chorus relies mostly on Apollo. These translations allow the reader to learn more about the events in Thebes as well as chorus.

It is through various poetic and rhetorical devices used by Grene and Fagles that allows the chorus to reveal more about the play. Grene's translation of the parados begins with the question "What is the sweet spoken word of God from the shrine of Pytho rich in gold that has come to glorious Thebes?" (151-152). By entering with this question, Grene illustrates the chorus's curiosity and uneasiness for their city. Similarly, Fagles begins the parados by presenting the chorus's curiosity, but with a series of specific questions: "Great welcome voice of Zeus, what do you bring?

What word from the gold vaults of Delphi comes to brilliant Thebes? (169-171). Fagles continues the questioning when the chorus calls to Apollo asking, "What is your price?" (174). Through these rhetorical questions, the chorus is shown as confused and wanting more information from the gods. Both translators use apostrophe throughout the speech, as the gods that the chorus calls to are not actually present in the scene. This presents credibility for the translators, as they are consistent with Sophocles's limitation of only being able to use so many characters at once. In the middle section of the chorus's speech, both Grene and Fagles catalog the present situation in Thebes when describing the people suffering from the plague and the many deaths that are occurring. By cataloging these events, the chorus is able to give details about the situation, but also to help move the plot along. With the help of these rhetorical devices, Grene and Fagles are able to provide detail about the play, yet advance the plot at the same time.

Both of the translations by David Greene and Robert Fagles present the chorus's confusion, anger, and determination through various rhetorical techniques and word choices. Even though the content of each of the speeches is the same, the context of Fagles's speech is much more appealing to the modern reader. The translator presents the chorus more as an individual than Grene as he details the actions and thoughts of the chorus through powerful diction and syntax. It seems in Grene's translation that the chorus is very cut and dry, only detailing the necessary parts of the story and not adding any of their feelings or emotion. The modern reader wants to be drawn into a story and be able to relate somewhat to the characters in it. Fagles achieves this through descriptive words choices and various punctuations. The chorus in *Oedipus the King* allows the reader to understand the current events in Thebes to help them make sense of the evolving story.

Works Cited

Fagles, Robert, and Bernard Knox. " Oedipus the King." *Sophocles. The Three ThebanPlays: Antigone, Oedipus the King, Oedipus at Colonus.* Trans. Robert Fagles. New York: Penguin Literature, 1984. Print.

Grene, David and Richmond Alexander Lattimore. "Oedipus the King." *Greek Tragedies.* Trans. David Grene. 2nd ed. Vol. 1. Chicago: University of Chicago, 1991. 117-19. Print.

Simplicated Aristotle

Patrick Lambdin

Throughout the works of Galileo, the reader does not directly communicate with the author but rather with three stylized characters: Sagredo, Salviati, and Simplicio. Sagredo, the sagacious inquisitor, and Salviati, a discerning scientist, are intelligent characters who take it in turn to argue for and question Galileo's own view of the universe. Simplicio, the dialogue's village idiot, advocates Aristotle's Earth-centered view of the universe. This paper discusses the presentation of arguments at the beginning of Galileo's *Dialogue Concerning the Two Chief World Systems*. First, the paper illustrates Galileo's rhetorical prowess at the beginning of the *Dialogue*. Next, the paper examines in a few examples how factors such as the speaker, specific placement of arguments, and the deliberate misquotation of Aristotle positively affect the potency of Galileo's propositions as well as Galileo's counter-arguments to Aristotle.

Before delving any deeper into Galileo's text one must be aware of the rhetoric both in Galileo's title as well as that within the first few pages of his work. The title itself, *Dialogue Concerning the Two Chief World Systems*, seems innocuous at first glance. However, there are several subtle rhetorical strategies even within these very first few words. The phrase *"Two Chief World Systems"* does not seem very suspicious to the present day reader— of course there are only the Copernican heliocentric cosmology which Galileo supports and Aristotle's terrestrially centered worldview. What may be difficult to realize however, is that the same title would have had the same effect on contemporary readers in Galileo's time. There were certainly more than *two* views about the arrangement of the solar system. Also, one should know that Galileo's picture of the universe was not the dominant theory of the time. Thus, Galileo's title creates a bias within the reader before the book has even been opened. This bias is that Galileo's ideas are at the very least on par with Aristotle's. The title also dismisses any number of alternative theories apart from Galileo and Aristotle's. In creating this kind of dualistic polemic, Galileo has eliminated the need to disprove any viewpoint other than that of an Aristotelian in order to have a complete monopoly on the way World Systems are envisioned.

Bearing in mind that Galileo judiciously chooses the words he uses in his writing to create a friendly bias in the reader, it is also worthwhile to carefully examine the first few pages of Galileo's *Dialogue*. It opens with Salviati laying out a blueprint of the ensuing dialogue and he makes more overt the rhetorical strategies present in the title.

Closely following Salviati's proem, there is a discussion of Aristotle's proof concerning the perfect nature of the Universe. Salviati claims, "The first step in the Peripatetic arguments is Aristotle's proof of the completeness and perfection of the world. For he tells us... it is a body having length width and depth. Since there are only these three dimensions, the world, having these, has them all, and, having the Whole, is perfect." (9). On the following page of the *Dialogue*, the word "three" appears numerous times as a characteristic which is both necessary and sufficient for perfection.] It does not seem much of a surprise that a dialogue published in Italy in the year 1632 opens with a discussion of the number three—the Trinity being one of the definitive marks of Christianity. What is unexpected is that Galileo questions whether three is a perfect number. Salviati even goes so far as to say, "To tell you the truth... I feel no compulsion to grant that the number three is a perfect number, nor do I feel that it has a power of conferring perfection upon its possessors." (11). He continues to say that the numbers two or four are no less perfect than the number three. Salviati offers legs as an example of the potential imperfection of the number three. For a person two legs are perfect. For a dog four legs are perfect. The number three is in no way perfect when applied to legs.

Surprisingly, Galileo opens his book exploring the order of heaven and earth and written for a heavily Catholic audience, including Vatican censors, with an apparent denouncement of the complete perfection of the number three. This sounds dangerous. Indeed, it proves to be dangerous for Galileo later when he was ordered to stand trial on suspicion of heresy and compelled to recant his book by the Church. Yet, it is a valuable point for the reader to note this. Because this passage shows that Galileo, as an author, is willing to order his text in an expected framework, but more than willing to fill this framework with unanticipated content.

Now, after seeing two of Galileo's tricks in their somewhat exposed form, one can look at Galileo's presentation of Aristotelian arguments. These syllogisms of Aristotle are primarily presented through the character Simplicio. Therefore, one must look carefully at Simplicio "that stout champion and defender of Aristotelian doctrines" (9).

Simplicio creates a large amount of bias against Aristotle in spite of the fact that he is Aristotle's advocate in the dialogue. The Italian's name is itself obviously related to the word "simple" which when applied to a human is often synonymous with "stupid". Simplicio is indeed stupid. Nearly every single one of his objections is easily explained away or politely glossed over by Sagredo and Salviati (11, 12, 14). Often Simplicio is asked very simple questions and upon answering correctly, receives an encouraging "Very good indeed!" from either Sagredo or Salviati (17). At one point of terminal confusion Simplicio says, "I shall not say that this argument of yours cannot be conclusive. But I still say, with Aristotle, that in physical matters one need not always require a mathematical demonstration." (14). Which equates to "I am not going to say anything. Aristotle says I don't need to know math." This quote which obviously ridicules Simplicio also ridicules Aristotle. It shows the reader that Simplicio does not know enough math to disprove Salviati. However, it also shows that Simplicio is willing to use Aristotle as a canvas on which to project his own inequities, making the Philosopher himself appear to be an imbecile. In short, Simplicio discredits any arguments which happen to emanate from his mouth—largely by virtue of his own stupidity.

The reader can now begin to see how important rhetoric is to Galileo. His title subtly places Mr. Galilei on equal footing with Aristotle while the character Simplicio discredits himself and Aristotle by being an idiot. Without having looked closely at any of Galileo's mathematical or scientific arguments against Aristotle, one can see that Aristotle has already lost most of the philosophical battle simply by virtue of Galileo's title and cast of characters. I say "Galileo's cast" inclusively because while Simplicio on the one hand discredits Aristotle, his idiocy simultaneously generates credibility for Sagredo and Salviati—and by extension Galileo. It is now clear that Galileo's rhetoric forms one of the strongest pillars of argumentation in his *Dialogue Concerning the Two Chief World Systems.*

Having seen that Galileo is capable of using effective rhetoric in his writing, let the reader now look closely at the substance of some of his arguments against an Aristotelian or Ptolemaic illustration of the Universe.

First, is an attack on the Aristotelian idea of motion. Sagredo begins the debate by challenging Aristotle's lack of a discussion of "rest" in *On the Heavens* (16). Sagredo then also challenges Aristotle's description of motion. Below is Aristotle's own definition of the magnitude of motion:

> All simple motion, then, must be motion either away from or towards or about the centre...But all movement that is in

place, all locomotion, as we term it, is either straight or circular or a combination of these two, which are the only simple movements. And the reason of this is that these two, the straight and the circular line, are the only simple magnitudes. (*On the Heavens* 2)

Sagredo's first complaint with this theory is that there are a number of circular objects in the universe making the ideas of "upward" and "downward" much more complicated. Sagredo says, "For I should say that in the real universe there are thousands of circular motions, and consequently thousands of centers, there would also be thousands of motions upward and downward." (16). Here, Sagredo challenges Aristotle's conclusions about absolute motion on the grounds that Aristotle was not in a position to make accurate cosmological predictions concerning motion. The Grecian philosopher's lack of ability to observe the universe from celestial spheres other than our own leads to the conclusion that the universe has only two directions of motion: up and down. Galileo realizes this fact. What Sagredo really states is that on *any* sphere, the entire Universe would appear to be characterized in the same way. Thus, there would be "thousands of motions upward and downward".[54]

The truly shrewd counter-example Galileo makes to disprove this Aristotelian proposition of motion is the inversion of the rule. For Aristotle claims, "All bodies are either simple or compounded... and that both movement of a simple body is simple and simple movement is of a simple body...." (*Heavens* 2). Sagredo pursues the idea that observing the motion can tell the observer out of what the moving object is made. He states, "Furthermore, if a greater or lesser velocity of motion can alter the simplicity of motion, no simple body would ever move with a simple motion, since in all natural straight motions the velocity is always increasing and consequently changing in simplicity." (17). In layman's terms: "If a rock gets faster as it falls, according to Aristotle, the rock is changing composition as it falls." This is a brilliant argument on Sagredo's part for a number of reasons.

First, it appears to reduce an Aristotelian understanding of natural motion to absurdity. However, below the level of appearances the discerning reader can once again see Galileo utilizing strong rhetoric. It is notably Simplicio not Aristotle who offers the hypothesis that *velocity* determines the composition of an object (17). In fact Aristotle himself is very vague about whether or not velocity enters into his definition or not. One could easily read Aristotle's definition as having only to do with the direction of motion regardless of velocity. Once again, Galileo cleverly seems to accomplish much without having actually done much. Sagredo has disproved only Simplicio's interpretation of Aristotle, not Aristotle's own definition. All Sagredo has done is to make *Simplicio* look stupid—not Aristotle. Through deliberate— albeit slight— misquotation as well as careful character

---

" Salviati agrees with this objection and it is discussed much more exhaustively on pages 34-38.

development, Galileo has once again used rhetorical strategies to carry the bulk of his argument.

Later Simplicio once again ruins Aristotle's chances of being taken seriously by anyone reading the *Dialogue*. On pages 34-36, Simplicio responds to questions posed by Salviati by refusing to entertain them. Motion and its true direction have once again been called into question by the two wise interlocutors. Their chief objection, as earlier, is that Aristotle did not consider the possibility that the motion observed relative Earth's surface is not the same as true "up" and "down" motion (36).

Simplicio seems to be genuinely offended saying things like, "This way of philosophizing tends to subvert all natural philosophy, and to disorder and set in confusion heaven and earth and the whole universe." (37). Of course if one examines this claim carefully he will see that subverting natural philosophy does not disorder the universe. Subverting natural philosophy only confuses the philosophers: not the heavens and the earth. Altering the way philosophers or scientists discuss physical objects does not change the objects themselves.

> Earlier, Simplicio makes an even more telling statement:
> There is no doubt whatever that since you wish to deny not only the principles of the science, but palpable experience and the very senses themselves, you can never be convinced nor relieved from any preconceived opinion. Therefore I shall hold my peace because *contra negantes principia non est disputandum*[55], and not because I am persuaded by your reasoning. (34)

---

[55] Against one who denies the principles, there can be no dispute.

This is a funny quotation. Who is the man actually refusing to listen to other arguments? Who cannot be convinced from *any* preconceived notion no matter the proofs of Sagredo and Salviati? The answer is obviously Simplicio. His defensive reply is at once ironic and false. Simplicio claims he shall hold his peace, but in fact continues speaking for the rest of the page. The Aristotelian, Simplicio, even *interrupts* Salviati after the scientist has said only two and half sentences in an attempted rebuttal.

However ironically funny this situation happens to be, one should wonder at why specifically Galileo chooses to have Simplicio remain so unapproachable throughout this scene. Simplicio's senseless babbling and his inability to argue effectively together neutralize the hope of any serious Aristotelian riposte. Galileo has Simplicio shoot off Aristotle's foot before the Philosopher has even walked into the room. This is done on purpose because Galileo knows that there is no physical proof of his own arguments involving perspective and absolute motion. A more intelligent Aristotelian would jump on this opportunity to attack the Italian. In any case, the genius of Galileo's rhetoric once again anticipates and eliminates any possible objection before it can be formed.

From the several pages above, one can now see that Galileo is a meticulous writer. He manipulates the thoughts of his readers through careful use of rhetoric. Beginning with the very title of his *Dialogue Concerning the Two World Systems*, Galileo mixes a cocktail of rhetorical strategies which persuade to agree with Galileo before opposing arguments can even begin to take place. These tricks include careful diction, deliberate misquotation, an intentional ambiguity between the speaker and the source the speaker is quoting, and using character traits to create biases for the different interlocutor's arguments. Any one of these wily deceptions can help to convince a reader. However, when all of these ruses are used cohesively and well used the reader will not even know that bias is being created. This paper reveals that behind the words and the complex mathematical arguments much of Galileo's persuasive force in the *Dialogue Concerning the Two World Systems* is simply Simplicio's simplicated Aristotle.

Bibliography

Galilei, Galileo. *Dialogue Concerning the Two Chief World Systems.* Translated by Drake, Stillman. London: University of California Berkely Press, 1981.

Aristotle. *On the Heavens.* Translated by: J.L. Shocks. From *Foundations of Natural Science Reader.* Collected by Brian Schwartz.

Paradise Seeking Paradise

Dana Ehrmann

The book entitled *On the Road*, which is Jack Kerouac's most popular novel, is one of the most aptly titled works in American literature. The piece in its entirety is either about traveling on the road or making plans to travel that way once again. However, it does not quite convey the ardor the band of main characters has for getting out and living their lives on both a literal and metaphorical journey. American society in the 1940s would soon harbor a desire to become completely stationary and commit all focus on attaining the American dream. During this period this period, the protagonist/narrator and his exuberant friends make their trek not just for kicks as they may often say, but to distance themselves from mainstream USA and society's expectations and obligations. The trips of Sal Paradise and Dean Moriarty, his effervescent pal, help to convey to the readers what their values are and, more often than not, are endeavors that are able to move them forward onto their next destination and eventually to the paradise they seek. It is on the road where they are happiest because the goal is to find a place free of the expectations they are evading. But the events that take place in the apparently perfect land they have found afterwards suggest that there is a time when their way of life must be set-aside for a more grounded one. In *On the Road*, the characters value traveling away from the society they know on their quest for paradise even if it kills them, and they do not care what they leave behind.

Sal's last name, "Paradise," is really the epitome of what he is searching for and what he considers important. Because it is an actual word serving as a pseudonym for the author himself, it suggests that the name was chosen deliberately as a symbol for his goal. Most normally think of "paradise" as Heaven, the most desirable place to go once one has perished. In this case, however, it likely means a place characterized by extreme peace and/or happiness, because Sal and his companions are not focused on dying, but living. They believe this place to be a physical destination, so they are in continual search for it. It is special because it does not follow the same social or legal guidelines as the society they live in. The car they drive around in for a great period of the time is a Cadillac, an American car representing American ideals of the time. As they get further along, the car sees a greater and greater state of disrepair and unappealing outward appearance. It is symbolic of the American dream fueling their quest, and crumbling down during their journey to find something better.

Driving across America brings the most bliss and vivacity to the characters' lives but at the same time, their adventure motoring through the country represents their literal and figurative mortality as well. After a night of stealing cars, Sal and Dean are trying to go on their way when Sal spots a police car: "Then we suddenly saw the cruiser coming and I knew it was the end of my life as I had known it and that it was entering a new and horrible stage..." (224). Here, it is made clear that their jaunt on the road could very easily end the same way by another vehicle on the road, a police car. The cruiser represents the ultimate authority that they do not want to be subjected to. "The man" and "the establishment" would keep them from living their carefree lives, so it makes sense that Sal sees this car as the end of his journey and the beginning of being confined to society's guidelines again; his apprehension mirrors his fear of being constrained to society's dictations. Then, though driving is the manner in which they fulfill their idea of living, it also brings them closer to their literal death. As the novel goes on, Dean drives more and more recklessly, sometimes playing games and racing with other drivers on the road. In relation to other cars, Sal comments: "He almost rammed them...I shuddered. I couldn't take it any more." Dean is so reckless that Sal is frightened for his life, and cannot look on as this destructive behavior takes place. Again, the thing that makes the likes of Sal and Dean feel so alive could also kill them. It proves how extreme their lifestyle really is and how close they are to having everything they want given to them, and taken away in the very same manner.

Sal and his friends constantly reveal their tendency to leave what they deem unimportant behind, which gives the reader insight into what it is that they do feel is essential in their lives. In an anecdote Sal tells about a time when his friend woke him up in the middle of the night during college, he says: "I got up and dropped some pennies on the floor when I put my pants on" (60).

The pennies are such a minute and ostensibly inconsequential detail to include in this account, but Kerouac uses it to convey that even in his younger days, money was not Sal's main concern. When he drops them, he does not pick them up because they are not one of the values that he holds dear. This directly relates to the way finances are handled throughout the novel; earning money is not a goal past attaining the amount needed for sustenance and transportation. It is spent uneconomically in some cases. The exception is in the purchasing of a car that will aid them on their journey. There is another moment when he says: "All my keys fell out; I never found them" (45). In reference to apartment keys, this shows Sal's lack of care for maintaining a residence. Multiple times, watches are sold for gas money, which signifies that he "undervalues time" and is "trading time for distance" (Shmoop Editorial Team, 2008). When Sal works as a security guard, he says that all he wants to do is: "...disappear somewhere, and go and find out what everybody was doing all over the country" (67). This is just one of the many examples that prove that steady employment is not a main focus. And, towards the end of the novel in Mexico, Sal becomes extremely ill, but even realizing that Dean leaves him. After all they had been through together travelling and getting to know each other very deeply, he leaves his friend sick in a foreign country without a second thought, because he feels he has to move on.

More alarmingly, it does not matter how deeply rooted in domestic life Sal or his friends seem to be, because they always end up abandoning who and what they have for the nomadic lifestyle they value more. Throughout the novel, Dean strings many women along. He marries his first wife, young Marylou, and stays with her sporadically. He spends the majority of his time either making love to her or carving out excuses to present to her so that he can go shack up with a different girl. Often times this other girl is Camille, his second wife and the mother of two of his children. When Camille gives birth to his first daughter, Dean settles down for a short time, and gives off the impression that he is content with his new life. But, as Sal narrates: "Then suddenly he blew his top while walking down the street one day. He saw a '49 Hudson for sale and rushed to the bank for his entire roll. He bought the car on the spot" (110-111). His desires were building up inside of him, while on the exterior he pretended to enjoy his family lifestyle. His impulsive buy reveals that he values a car that allows him to follow his dreams more than any amount of money or his family. At a certain point later, it looks as though the idea of the American dream has grown on Dean once more, and that it has wrangled his restless soul and convinced it to settle down again. He describes his baby daughter: "...my terrific darling beautiful daughter can now stand alone for thirty seconds at a time..." (186) His use of three consecutive sparkling adjectives proves how much he adores his daughter. Also, the fact that he is bragging about her ability to simply stand alone, as all babies eventually learn to do, shows how he has become a proud parent. Yet immediately after this bit of dialogue appears, Sal says in his narration: "And in the morning Camille threw both of us out, baggage and all" (186). It was because they had called up an old friend and wanted to go out and get drunk. That Camille threw their baggage out along with them signifies the finality of their separation. There is not an absence of love for family displayed here, but love is not enough to tie Sal or Dean down, because it does not propel them forward. This idea applies to Dean abandoning another girl he impregnated, Inez, and also Sal being able to leave his love Terry and her son, whom he has grown quite fond of. Ed Dunkel, the chum of the two, marries a girl named Galatea. When Dean comes around and excites him with the thought of going out on the road, they actually ditch her in a motel lobby, because she is slowing them down and her desires do not match theirs. These men can only be stationary for so long before they get the itch to move on and have new experiences. Ultimately, their relationships hold them back from their adventures.

On one side, Sal and his friends represent the exciting youth who live their lives the way they want to rather than how society dictates. On the other hand, they treat the people they love badly, and sometimes it is easy to think of them as having no purpose or contribution to the betterment of society. Ultimately, Kerouac seems to be saying with the culmination of his work that it is a beautiful, thrilling, and energizing thing to do what his characters have done, but there is a time in one's life when that dream has to end. Mexico shows all the signs of being the paradise Sal is looking for. However, that changes when he gets sick and

Dean leaves him behind. In the very end, Sal has a steady girlfriend. The last time he sees Dean, he is about to go to a concert, and cannot spend the time with him that Dean wants. He says: "...the only thing I could do was sit in the back of the Cadillac and wave at him" (309). Sal is riding in a Cadillac, which proves that he has reached the point in his life where he is revisiting the idea of the American dream, and is more open to it. The phase of his life that he spends traveling is over.

Works Cited

Kerouac, Jack. *On the Road*. Dallas: Penguin, 1957. Print.

Shmoop Editorial Team. "Watches in On the Road" *Shmoop.com*. Shmoop University, Inc., 11 Nov. 2008. Web. 29 Apr. 2012.

Donning the Dappled Fawnskin: Imitation within Euripides' *Bacchae*

John (Nick) Tackes

Euripides' *Bacchae* presents a glimpse into the lives and struggles of the god Dionysus, his worshippers, and Pentheus, the prince of Thebes. Dionysus wants to establish his rites in Thebes, yet he must compete with Pentheus for its affection. The god's worshippers, called the Bacchae, find themselves caught in the crossfire. To fulfill their respective desires, these characters adorn themselves in similar costumes of dappled fawnskin and ivy creepers, and thereby engage in imitation. By the end of the tragedy, these three characters realize three very different fates. The success or failure of Dionysus, Pentheus, and the Bacchae, both in imitation and in the ability to fulfill their desires, illustrates their need to cope with being drawn in two different directions: toward individuality and toward commonality. The manner by which these characters pursue their desires sheds light on the tension between individuality and commonality, and also highlights how imitation mediates those elements. Ultimately, the fates of Dionysus, Pentheus, and the Bacchae reveal that although divinities can resolve the irreconcilability between individuality and commonality, mortals cannot, and must either find means to cope with the tension or be torn apart by it.[56]

---

[56] All references to the text reference: Euripides. *Bacchae*. Translated and edited by Stephen Joseph. Esposito. Newburyport, Ma.: Focus Pub./R Pullins, 1998. Print.

I. Dionysus: Effeminate Interlocutor

Dionysus' overarching desire will be identified before analyzing how and why he imitates the Bacchic model of dappled fawnskin and ivy creepers. In the opening lines of the play Dionysus explains, "I first came to this Greek city... so that I might be seen by mortals as a god" (20). He repeats his intent when he specifies: "I must vindicate my mother Semele by revealing myself to mortals as the god whom she bore to Zeus" (41). Two additional elements explain Dionysus' desire in greater detail: the controversial love affair between his mother Semele and Zeus, and his previous exploits throughout Asian lands. These two elements demonstrate that Dionysus engages in imitation because he realizes that to successfully reveal himself to Thebes, he must implement less-than-direct tactics.

Dionysus mentions that the flames surrounding his mother's tomb are "a memorial of Hera's undying hybris" (9). This claim suggests that Dionysus' perception of his mother's death follows a particular account of Zeus and Semele in which Hera convinced Semele to ask Zeus to appear in his full glory. Zeus did so, but his revelation killed Semele since he took the form of a lightning strike. In other words, even though Semele wished to see Zeus and fully appreciate his divine nature, the revelation of his godhead overpowered her because of her mortality. Dionysus' reference to this event highlights a theme of mortal recognition of godhead present throughout the tragedy. The danger of the direct revelation of godhead exists as a fresh memory in Thebes, for Dionysus says, "I see the tomb of my thunder-struck mother here near the palace and the fallen ruins of her house smouldering with the still living flames of Zeus' blast" (6). The still living flames signify that Semele's death has not been forgotten, especially by Dionysus. He acknowledges his mother's death as a failed attempt to recognize divinity in its unadulterated form, as well as the fatal nature of such attempts. Dionysus understands the significance of Semele's fate, which explains why he takes the specific measures he does to reveal his godhead to Thebes.

Dionysus' previous exploits throughout Asia show that the god understands how to successfully make his godhead known to humans. Dionysus notes: "I first came to this Greek city only after I had roused to dancing all those Asian lands and established my rites there so that I might be seen by mortals as a god" (20). To rouse Asia into dancing seems a much "gentler" tactic than to appear in unfiltered divinity as a lightning strike. The term "gentler" adequately explains how Dionysus' approach to revelation differs from the way Zeus manifested his godhead to Semele. To rouse others to dancing does not present a raw source of power or divinity, but instead allows for a participative experience in which mortals can spiritually feel the deity and remain alive. The ecstatic nature of dance allows participants to step "outside of self," and experience oneness with something apart from themselves: in this case, Dionysus. Dionysus made a conscious effort to avoid the dangers of divine revelation to mortals when he established his godhead in Asia through dance. More convincing, perhaps, is that Dionysus compelled the Asians to don Bacchic apparel. The ivy, oak, evergreen creepers, and dappled fawnskin worn by the Bacchae throughout the tragedy are associated with the vestments and worship of Dionysus (12, 24, 35, 105, 175, 205, 249, 342). When the Asians wear the apparel that likens them to the god, they worship him. Imitation serves to help the Asian followers realize Dionysus' divinity, for it brings the deity and follower closer together without destroying the latter. Therefore, when Dionysus mentions both Semele's fate and his past exploits throughout Asia, he demonstrates an understanding of how to reveal himself to mortals safely and successfully.

After his speech at the beginning of the tragedy, Dionysus attempts to rouse Thebes to dancing by summoning the chorus of Bacchae to dance through the streets. When they do so, the Bacchae explicitly call Thebes to join in the revelry: "O Thebes... Abound, abound... rave with Bacchic frenzy" (105). However, the memory of Semele in the city marks a major difference between Dionysus' past Asian audience and his present Theban audience. Dionysus must face a city whose perception of Semele's death suggests that he is not a god. During his opening speech Dionysus declares, "my mother's sisters, of all people, denied that I, Dionysus, was begotten by Zeus" (27). He also mentions that Pentheus opposes him: "But that one, Pentheus, fights against the gods by fighting against me" (44). And indeed, Pentheus does reject Dionysus' divinity. Among Pentheus' first words in the tragedy, he proclaims, "The truth is that Dionysus was incinerated by fiery lightning along with his mother Semele because she had lied about her union wih Zeus" (244). Because of the strong opposition to his divinity, Dionysus must prepare to use a more aggressive means to establish his rites in Thebes than he did throughout Asia. Dionysus declares that, "this city must learn well, even if it doesn't want to learn, that it is still uninitiated in my Bacchic rites" (39). Despite Dionysus' forceful tone, the "gentle" element of his approach remains. Dionysus does not appear to Thebes in an unbridled divine manifestation. Instead, he imitates a mortal man, referred to as the Stranger, who can mingle within the social groups of Thebes and the Bacchae without destroying them. Upon first glance, Dionysus' choice to imitate a mortal bacchant does not make sense. After all, Pentheus persecutes the Bacchae for sexual promiscuousness, and the Stranger's provocative appearance makes him out to be a participant in the debauchery. It would appear that by donning the dappled fawnskin, Dionysus asks only for trouble. However, Dionysus' Bacchic garb has two distinct advantages. First, Dionysus is able to use his apparel to earn credibility among the other Bacchae. For example, the Bacchae recognize him as one of their own. When the Stranger is imprisoned, they lament: "Already [Pentheus] detains my fellow-reveller inside the palace" (547). Through the Stranger, Dionysus gains the ability to communicate with his worshippers effectively. This ability, as will be seen, aids Dionysus in revealing his godhead. The second advantage of Dionysus' imitation of a bacchant is that he ensures a face-to-face confrontation with Pentheus. Although this at first appears a disadvantage, Dionysus has nothing to fear from Pentheus; after all, Dionysus is a god and Pentheus is a mortal. Because Pentheus recognizes the Stranger as the leader of the Bacchae, he goes out of his way to detain and interrogate the effeminate man (352). The dialogues between Pentheus and the Stranger make up a large part of the tragedy, and within them Dionysus is able to goad Pentheus to the destruction that ultimately leads to Thebes' recognition of Dionysus' divinity.

By assuming a mortal form Dionysus is able to interact directly with Pentheus to achieve the recognition he ultimately desires from Thebes. In his mortal guise, Dionysus drops hints of his divinity to Pentheus, which "sets the stage" for Dionysus' final revelation at the end of the tragedy. When Pentheus asks why the Stranger brings his rites to Thebes, the Stranger responds: "Dionysus himself, the son of Zeus, sent me" (466). At one point Pentheus asks the Stranger what form the god took. The Stranger alludes to the divinity of Dionysus when he replies, "Whatever form he wanted" (478). Pentheus fails to acknowledge this, and retorts, "Very clever, these empty-worded evasions of yours" (479). The Stranger's comments intimate that Dionysus really is a deity and should be respected and honored as one, yet are phrased to keep Pentheus opposed to the idea. Dionysus cunningly uses the Stranger's human form to provoke Pentheus, and compels Pentheus to weave himself into a position where he deserves harsh punishment for rejecting Dionysus' divinity. This punishment, upon its execution, leaves Thebes with the brutal truth that Dionysus is a god. In short, the imitation that Dionysus engages in allows for him to fulfill desire to be recognized a god by Thebes.

Dionysus' ability to converse with the Bacchae through imitation also aids him in his divine revelation. Just after Pentheus imprisons the Stranger, Dionysus appears as a disembodied voice accompanied by an earthquake and lightning strike. When he does so, Dionysus comes close to using an unbridled manifestation to establish his godhead, despite his knowledge of its dangers. However, Dionysus uses his mortal form, the Stranger, to "soften the blow," so to speak. By using the Stranger to explain his manifestation, the god effectively allows his followers to experience a glimpse of his true divine power. Dionysus' manifestation threatens to destroy Pentheus' palace in the fury of lightning and earthquakes, and his Bacchae fear the occurrence. They shout among each other: "Throw your trembling bodies to the ground... For the king, Zeus' son, will come rushing upon this house, turning it upside down" (600). Dionysus retains an element of mystery and distance since he lacks visible form outside of the rumbling fire and chaos provided by earthquakes and lightning strikes. The nature of his appearance makes it difficult for his followers to understand the significance of the event. The danger associated with the phenomena, coupled with the lack of a visible source, makes him both threatening and unapproachable. However, Dionysus has his mortal incarnation explain the phenomena to the Bacchae. Although they are afraid of the destructive episode, the reassuring words of the Stranger bring the Bacchae from their fearful posture. He tells the Bacchae, "Women of Asia are you so paralyzed with fear that you've fallen to the ground... Come on, lift up your bodies! Take Courage! Cast off your trembling!" to which the Bacchae respond, "O greatest light of our Bacchic revelry! Euoi! How delighted I am to see you!" (604). Dionysus gains the ability to converse with his followers through imitation, and by doing so he stabilizes his otherwise unbridled manifestation. The comforting words of the Stranger allow Dionysus to make his godhead understandable to the Bacchae.

Dionysus' successful use of imitation largely relies upon his divinity. He knows that Thebes is fated to recognize him as a god, and makes it clear to Cadmus that "Long ago Zeus, my father, assented to these things" (1349). Because of his divinity, Dionysus is also exempt from defeat by his mortal enemies, namely Pentheus. Throughout the play, Dionysus deftly evades Pentheus' efforts to subordinate him, both in dialogue and in action. After escaping from Pentheus' palace he tells his Bacchae, "Calmly leaving the palace, I have come to you, giving no thought to Pentheus" (636). In addition, Dionysus has an advantage over mortals in that he is not bound or restricted by human limitations. He simultaneously appears in two distinct forms, which mortals cannot do: his awful manifestation as a disembodied voice accompanied by lighting and an earthquake, and the Stranger, who can explain the first form to others. Finally, since he ultimately wants to be recognized a god, Dionysus' imitation does not have to be foolproof. Thebes saw the Stranger and perceived that he was a mortal whose miracles pointed to the legitimacy of Dionysus' godhead. However, if Thebes saw through Dionysus' mortal disguise and recognized him as a god, Dionysus' desire would have been fulfilled that much faster. All of the advantages of Dionysus' divinity allow him to imitate safely and successfully, and this imitation in turn allows him to convince Thebes that he is a god. The mortal characters in the play do not share in Dionysus' success, however. Pentheus struggles with imitation, and his failure to imitate others ultimately ends in dismemberment at the hands of his mother, Agave.

II. Pentheus: In Stubborn Solitude

Pentheus and Dionysus share parallel desires, for both characters hope to earn the recognition of Thebes: Dionysus wishes to be recognized as a god, and Pentheus wishes to be recognized as an able leader. Pentheus' words and actions showcase his desire to earn recognition as the leader of Thebes. He believes that an impure influence plagues the city, and he acts as though ridding Thebes of this plague will grant him the recognition he desires. When Pentheus steps onstage for the first time, he vividly describes the state of the city to Cadmus, Pentheus' grandfather and the founder of Thebes, and Tiresias, the aged and revered seer of the city: "our women have abandoned their homes for the sham revelries of Bacchus... to service the lusts of men" (216). He also professes that he feels a sense of duty to put a stop to such evils by imprisoning the frenzied women and beheading their leader, the Stranger: "I've shackled with chains all those I've captured and thrown them into the public jails... I'll put a stop to [their leader]... In fact I'll cut his head right off his body!" (226-241). Pentheus relates the evildoings of the Bacchae as well as the punishments he has planned for them with forceful description and detail, and he crafts his speech to leave a strong impression on both Cadmus and Tiresias. Pentheus' remarks display his desire to preserve the order and normalcy of the *polis*, as well as making him out to be someone capable of ridding Thebes of its affliction. Because Pentheus' audience is comprised of Cadmus and Tiresias, the vivacity of Pentheus' speech holds special importance. Both old men are among the city's most respected figures. It is pragmatic to earn recognition from the city elders and become recognized as a capable and respectable leader in the eyes of the rest of the *polis*. If the most respected individuals in the city support the actions of Pentheus, the public's high esteem of such respected people will compel them to respect Pentheus as well. Pentheus' forceful description of the corrupted state of the city, his promise to be the one to fix it, and the presence of Cadmus and Tiresias suggest that Pentheus is acutely aware of how others perceive him. His opening remarks show that he desires to be viewed and respected as the leader of Thebes.

Throughout the *Bacchae*, various characters react to Pentheus' behavior and emphasize that he has a tendency to separate himself from others. Pentheus' own messenger fears his violent and haughty nature: "I fear the swiftness of your mind, my lord; it is quick to anger and too much that of a king" (670). The messenger's remark that Pentheus' mind is too kingly emphasizes just how removed Pentheus is from the rest of Thebes. He is "too much a king," to the extent where others do not want to interact with him. Even Cadmus asks Pentheus to abandon his anger. Cadmus perceives that Pentheus tends to operate upon his own volitions, and advises Pentheus to join with him and Tiresias: "My son, Tiresias has advised you well. Live with us rather than outside the law" (330). However, Pentheus reacts angrily at this suggestion: "Get your hand away from me!" and then orders his guards to dismantle Tiresias' abode (343). His reactions betray a stubborn nature and a tendency to pull away from others. Rather than cede any of his individuality and cooperate, Pentheus remains alone.

Pentheus makes a show of his authoritative role in his attempts to restore Thebes to order. He employs various soldiers and messengers to carry out his tasks for him, which further demonstrates his will to stand apart from the rest of the society. Messengers periodically report to Pentheus the outcomes of various missions that he has sent them on, which signifies the public nature of Pentheus' exploits. One soldier reports that, "The Theban Bacchae whom you shut up and seized and bound in chains at the public jail, those women are gone, let loose and skipping off, off to the mountain meadows, calling out to Bromios their god" (434). Pentheus delegates tasks to subordinates who willingly carry out his affairs, and he also receives aid from

Thebans who weren't ordered by him at all. A messenger reports an occurrence that happened to his fellow herdsmen and himself: "Some wanderer from the city with a knack for words spoke to us all: 'O you who dwell in the holy uplands of the mountains, do you wish to hunt Agave... and gain the king's favor?'" (717). The messenger's report shows that knowledge of Pentheus' mission reaches even beyond the city limits. Another messenger who had accompanied Pentheus into the mountains relates Pentheus' dismemberment to the chorus (1044). The messenger highlights the public nature of Pentheus' exploits, even after Pentheus' death. When Pentheus delegates tasks to his subordinates he expresses his will to be recognized as an authority figure. Pentheus' attempt to purge Thebes of its evils is a public affair, and it aligns with his desire to appear in command.

Pentheus' leadership differs from the leadership seen among the Bacchae, as will later be shown. Agave leads the Bacchae, but in every instance she calls the rest of the Bacchae to act with her in collective action. There is no delegation or distance between her and her comrades. Pentheus' leadership, however, results in his separation from the rest of Thebes. His approach is direct and his orders are snappy. He desires to distinguish himself from his mortal peers and to appear godlike before the city, as opposed to the Bacchae whose leader acts with them and as one of them. Pentheus' approach also differs from the way Dionysus attempts to make his godhead known. Dionysus tries to minimize the distance between himself and his followers. He uses the

Stranger to intermingle and care for his followers, and the Stranger is only recognized a leader insofar as he is able to interpret the god's actions. While Dionysus and Agave remain closely attached to those they lead, Pentheus pulls away. He distances himself from Thebes, and clings to his distinction as an authority figure.

Pentheus displays stubborn and violent behavior whenever he faces opposition or feels threatened by others. These reactions betray his unwillingness to appear overpowered or without control. Pentheus' explosive reactions leave strong impressions upon those who see him. In response to Pentheus' orders to ransack Tiresias' home, the seer claims that "Pentheus is a fool and says foolish things" (369). Tiresias perceives the brash reaction of Pentheus and comments on the violence of the prince's remarks. The chorus of Bacchae lament: "Do you hear these words of Pentheus? Do you hear his hybris, blaspheming Bromios, Semele's son... ?" (374). Their comments demonstrate the perception that Pentheus reacts with pride. The Stranger also warns Pentheus of the dangers of his tendency towards stubborn, hubristic violence: "I would sacrifice to [Dionysus] rather than rage on, kicking against the pricks, a man at war with god" (794). From virtually all fronts Pentheus is accosted and warned that his violent and stubborn behavior will lead to no good, and that it works against his ability to earn the respect and honor of Thebes. His reactions differ greatly from the "gentle" approach used by Dionysus. Pentheus does not wish to use any gentleness at all. Since he is a mortal attempting to stand out from a crowd which he closely resembles already, Pentheus wants to appear somewhat godlike, to avoid blending into the common public, and to act upon his own volitions rather than upon the advice of others. For these reasons he continually attempts to distance himself from other people.

Pentheus' uncompromising hubris prevents others' advice from taking hold, and instead he incorrectly perceives that his authority alone will allow him to achieve Thebes' respect. Pentheus is concerned with authority. Advice appears as a threat to such authority. He reacts to advice with violence out of fear, for his desire to possess recognition as the leader of Thebes turns all external suggestions into threats to his authority and independence. Upon seeing Tiresias, Pentheus accuses him of "importing... sinister rituals" (260). He later orders his soldiers to "tear [Tiresias' abode] up with crowbars" (352). Whether or not Pentheus believes that Tiresias truly imported the rituals is irrelevant: Pentheus perceives Tiresias as a threat to his desire to earn recognition as the leader of Thebes. Pentheus attempts to remove the high public opinion of Tiresias and to replace him as a figurehead of the city. In his view, the sight of soldiers marching through town to vandalize Tiresias' home would leave a strong impression upon the Theban populace: it would highlight Pentheus' authority and diminish Tiresias' reputation. Pentheus quickly resorts to violence as a means to address his perceived threat, which leaves little room for any sort of compromise or civilized discourse. He showcases a desire to undermine the reputations of the city's respected individuals, and does so in a manner that lets the public know of his status as a leader.

Pentheus reacts to the Stranger through a similar course of action. Pentheus orders his guards to bind the Stranger, and directly challenges the Stranger's authority by saying "I have more power than you!" (505). Pentheus draws attention to his own authoritative position and belittles the Stranger. His outburst illustrates his sensitivity toward any perceived threat to his leadership status. Pentheus intends to execute the Stranger publically, for he tells his guards to capture him "so that he's brought to justice by being stoned to death" (356). Pentheus wills to turn all threats into examples of his authority by removing them in a violent and public manner. He wishes to use such absolute methods to convince Thebes that he is a capable leader. Pentheus' behavior strays away from the humane and contains little to no sympathy. It highlights his perception of what it means to act with authority. When compared to Dionysus' methods it becomes clear that the two characters use opposite means to achieve like ends: Dionysus imitates human behavior to achieve his recognition as a god, whereas Pentheus imitates godlike behavior – at least in his own eyes – to achieve recognition as a leader.

The Stranger's presence in Thebes threatens Pentheus on multiple levels. For Pentheus to receive the recognition that he desires from Thebes, he must perceive that the city is intact and healthy. Pentheus expresses contempt for the lewd behavior of the Bacchae. Even if Pentheus perceived that a morally bankrupt

Thebes showered him with respect and admiration, he would not honor that respect due to the contemptibility of the people. Pentheus desires to maintain a healthy *polis* not only because he wishes to earn the respect of the Theban citizens, but because he wishes to receive such respect from a legitimate and respectable populace. Pentheus believes the leader of the Bacchae tempts the Theban women away from proper behavior and custom: he states that "this effeminate looking stranger... brings a new disease to the women and dishonors their beds!" (353). The Stranger threatens Pentheus' ability to achieve the respect of what he considers to be a morally-sound city. Not only does the Stranger threaten to steal the respect of the Theban citizens, but he also threatens to transform the respect of the Theban populace into a detestable object to Pentheus.

Pentheus' concern with Thebes' moral standing shows that Thebes must remain somewhat similar to his perception of a proper city to fulfill his desire. Not only must Pentheus tailor his behavior to the degree necessary for the city to perceive him as a distinct and respectable leader, but he must also act as a model of propriety for Thebes to imitate. Because Pentheus expresses that he wishes to save Thebes from the corrupt behavior of the Bacchae, and because he wants to exist as the model for Thebes' proper behavior, Pentheus is extremely reluctant to engage in anything he perceives shameful. When the Stranger proposes that Pentheus should dress up in Bacchic apparel, Pentheus initially protests, "In what kind of costume? A woman's? But I would be ashamed." (821). Pentheus fears association with the effeminate nature of the Stranger, for he views the Stranger as a threat to the moral sanctity of Thebes. Pentheus wishes to avoid the same behavior that he perceives signifies the moral corruption of the Theban women. However, Pentheus ultimately does dress in the female costume of the Bacchae. Before understanding why he follows through with something he considers shameful, a few prior events must be explained.

Pentheus does not imitate the Bacchae until he realizes that he cannot defeat Dionysus using only his own devices. Just before Dionysus' first dialogue with Pentheus, Pentheus perceives that Dionysus has succeeded in earning Thebes' respect. A soldier explains the circumstances of Dionysus' capture: "[Dionysus] even stood still so as to make my task easy. Feeling ashamed I said to him: 'Stranger, not willingly do I arrest you but by the orders of Pentheus who sent me'" (439). The soldier's sense of shame when following Pentheus' orders signifies that the soldier regrets obeying Pentheus and sympathizes with Dionysus. Rather than confronting the soldier about his disposition toward Dionysus, Pentheus engages in a dialogue with the Stranger. Pentheus attempts to display his worthiness as a leader to his soldier while simultaneously belittling Dionysus. Pentheus ends the dialogue when he orders his soldiers to imprison Dionysus, and claims "I order them to bind you. I have more power than you!" (505). Pentheus is clearly aware of the power struggle between Dionysus and himself, yet still stubbornly refuses to acknowledge that he cannot win against the Stranger.

The Stranger's arrest gives cause to reflect on an important distinction between the tactics of Dionysus and those of Pentheus, for Pentheus' stubbornness undermines his ability to earn Thebes' respect. By contrast, the Stranger behaves with compliance and good grace among the Thebans – he does not resist the soldier who arrests him, nor does he belittle him or ridicule him. Because of his acquiescence, the Stranger wins over and fascinates Pentheus' soldier. The soldier admits to Pentheus that, "This man has come here to Thebes full of many miracles" (449). Were Pentheus out of the picture, it appears as though the soldier would have no quarrel with the Stranger and would even believe in Dionysus' divinity due to the Stranger's miracles. By contrast, Pentheus' stubborn nature alienates his soldier from the purpose of his orders. The soldier expresses his lack of concern for Pentheus' cause when he tells the Stranger, "not willingly do I arrest you" (441). In addition, he never mentions the Bacchic affliction on Thebes that Pentheus raves about. After arresting the Stranger, the soldier instead tells Pentheus that, "what happens next must be your concern, not mine" (450). This episode shows that Pentheus' stubbornness does harm to the respect he receives from Thebes, and that Dionysus' willingness to comply grants him a degree of influence over the soldier's estimation of him.

Pentheus' continual striving to distinguish himself from the common public lessens when he can no longer ignore his repeated shortcomings. Pentheus fails to subdue Dionysus and his followers. The same soldier who brings the Stranger to Pentheus admits that the Bacchae escaped from prison (443). Soon after his imprisonment, the Stranger escapes from Pentheus' palace (642). After that, Pentheus' men are forced to flee from the violent frenzy of the Bacchae (735). These events threaten Pentheus' reputation. The public of Thebes would see Pentheus' repeated failure to restrain the Stranger and his Bacchae, and their perception of his ability to lead them would diminish. After all of these failed attempts, Pentheus ceases to try to imprison the Stranger and instead begins to take his advice. When the Stranger escapes from imprisonment, Pentheus shifts his countenance from hostility to compliance. Pentheus admits to the Stranger: "You're a pretty clever fellow and have been right all along" (824). The Stranger then persuades Pentheus to dress as one of the Bacchae to spy on them. Although reluctant at first, Pentheus ultimately agrees to imitate the Bacchae. It seems he feels that successfully spying on them will serve his larger desire to earn the respect of Thebes. It is unclear how Pentheus feels spying will provide him with an advantage in his desire to be respected and honored by Thebes. However, evidence shows that he believes it will.

Pentheus' remarks throughout his dialogue with the Stranger show that his decision-making relies heavily upon his desire to be respected by the Theban populace. At several points during his dialogue with the Stranger, Pentheus remarks that he does not want to be recognized in shameful guise. He calls the

Stranger's advice into question: "What are you saying? Instead of being a man shall I join the ranks of women?" (822). He responds to the Stranger's persistence: "In what kind of costume? A woman's? But I would be ashamed" (828). After even more urging by the Stranger, Pentheus states "I couldn't bear to put on a female costume" (836). Pentheus repeatedly resists the Stranger's advice because he fears it will jeopardize the attainment of his desire. Pentheus wants to remain undetected while in his female costume, and before he agrees to go along with the Stranger's advice he must feel that his reputation is safe. Pentheus fears that Thebes will interpret his costume as admittance of his errors and an acceptance of Dionysus as a god because he has already made it publically known that he holds the Bacchae in contempt. Pentheus states: "how will I avoid the notice of the Cadmeans as I pass through the city?" (840). Pentheus is reluctant to cede any of his individuality to achieve his ultimate goal. He keeps his desire to remain respectable to Thebes in mind when he decides whether or not to imitate one of the Bacchae, which shows that he wants to stay true to his perception of proper behavior. At the end of the dialogue, Pentheus remains hesitant: "I'll do the deciding about what seems best... for either I will march with weapons or I'll obey [the Stranger's] advice" (843). His ultimate choice to dress in Bacchic apparel signifies that he believes it will help him earn recognition as a leader of Thebes, but more importantly shows that he has begun to relinquish some of his individuality to serve his larger desire.

By dressing up a bacchant, Pentheus becomes less and less like himself. However, he cannot completely abandon his will to remain respectable in the eyes of Thebes, which undermines his ability to successfully spy on the Bacchae. Pentheus expresses interest in looking just like a bacchant. He asks Dionysus: "Don't I carry myself like Ino or like Agave, my mother?" (925). And again: "Will I look more like a bacchant if I hold the thyrsus in my right hand or here, in my left?" (941). The very act of spying suggests that Pentheus does not want the Bacchae to be able to distinguish him from the rest of their social group. However, Pentheus still wants the Thebans to be able to view his bravery as he marches to the mountain in his guise. Pentheus commands Dionysus: "Escort me through the main streets of Thebes. For I am the only man of all the Thebans to dare this" (961). Even when attempting to assume a female guise, Pentheus will not completely abandon his masculine identity, nor will he abandon his care for how Thebes perceives him. Pentheus' decision to dress as a bacchant to spy on the Bacchae only takes him so far. Because he believes imitation will help fulfill his desire to cure Thebes of its affliction and thereby achieve recognition as a leader, Pentheus becomes less and less like himself. But he cannot completely transform into one of the Bacchae. Pentheus' obsession with earning Thebes' respect prevents him from truly assuming the form of his enemies, even if only to spy on them.

Since he fails to cede enough of his individuality, even temporarily, Pentheus dies at the hands of the Bacchae he tries to imitate. Even in his final moments, Pentheus ascends a fir tree rather than mingling among the Bacchae (1073). In other words, Pentheus refrains from joining into the Bacchic group even after dressing as a bacchant, which allows the Bacchae to identify him as an outsider. Rather than taking additional steps toward assimilation into the group of Bacchae, Pentheus keeps his distance, which ultimately destroys him. His final words show that, even in his dying breaths, Pentheus cannot part with his identity. He implores Agave: "It is I, mother, your son Pentheus to whom you gave birth in the house of Echion" (1118). Rather than trying to fit in as a bacchant, Pentheus persists in holding onto his identity as Agave's son. Despite his attempt to make his identity known, Agave tears Pentheus apart with her bare hands (1122). She does not recognize him either as one of the Bacchae or as her son, but rather as a "mounted beast" (1108). Pentheus' destruction at his mother's hands highlights his failed imitation.

Pentheus does not properly understand his limits, which partially explains his failure. Throughout the early part of the play, both Tiresias and Dionysus make comments that show a weakness in Pentheus - he does not understand himself or his personal limitations. Tiresias warns Pentheus, "Don't be so sure that force is what dominates human affairs, nor if you have an opinion but that opinion is sick, imagine that your opinion makes you somehow wise" (310). Tiresias implies that Pentheus should not be so sure of himself, and that he is not as smart as he thinks he is. Dionysus makes a more direct comment to Pentheus just before Pentheus imprisons him: "You don't know what your life is – neither what you're doing nor who you are" (506). These warnings make Pentheus out to be a character without proper understanding of how he fits into the world, which explains the inner tension he experiences throughout the tragedy. Pentheus struggles because he desires to distinguish himself as a leader without knowing the best means to do so. His messengers view him as "too much a king," and he inevitably becomes alienated from the very city he desires to lead. His flawed perception of himself, his capabilities, and the proper relationship between ruler and ruled prevent Pentheus from achieving his desire.

Pentheus' stubborn individuality forces him into direct conflict with a god, which inevitably points to Pentheus' defeat. Pentheus' stubbornness creates a situation in which the success of his desire hinges upon Dionysus' failure. If Pentheus achieves the recognition he desires as the leader of Thebes, Dionysus must not be honored by the public. Pentheus maintains that Dionysus' revelries are morally bankrupt, and considers those who engage in the worship of Dionysus to be shameful. Pentheus' desire allows for no compromise in this regard, for he would hold those who honored Dionysus through Bacchic behavior in contempt. Similarly, Pentheus' stubbornness forces the success of Dionysus' desire to hinge upon Pentheus' destruction. If Dionysus achieves recognition as a god, Pentheus cannot remain in the city, let alone lead it. Pentheus' public display of disgust for Bacchic revelry, his stubborn and violent nature, and his desire for the undivided respect of Thebes prevents him from any potential acceptance of Dionysus' divinity. His vision of the city does not contain worship of Dionysus anywhere within it. Rather, Pentheus would have the populace of Thebes share his view of Dionysus. If Thebes recognized Pentheus as their respected leader, Pentheus would take measures to distance the Theban populace from Bacchic behavior and instead behave according to Pentheus' idea of propriety. The citizens would not worship Dionysus, nor would they want to. For Thebes to accept Dionysus as a god Pentheus must either be destroyed or, at the very least, not taken seriously. Thebes could honor Dionysus as a deity and regard Pentheus as a fool, or they could be rid of him as a means to worship Dionysus in peace. In either case, the success of Dionysus' recognition as a deity depends upon Pentheus' failed attempt to secure the respect of the Theban populace.

Because of the direct and incorrigible opposition between Dionysus and Pentheus, Pentheus' failure becomes inevitable. Unlike Dionysus, Pentheus is a mere mortal. He does not have the means to utilize multiple forms – one common to the social group and one distinct from it – to achieve his desire through imitation. Dionysus does not have cause to worry about defeat by human powers – he is a god, after all. Rather, Dionysus must only find a way for Thebes to recognize his godhead without completely destroying the city upon his revelation. Pentheus, on the other hand, is mortal, and must take care to preserve his physical being. As was mentioned, Pentheus does not understand his limitations.

Being recognized as a leader seduces Pentheus to show off his personal abilities while rejecting the advice of others. His desire to stand out leaves him vulnerable and without support. Unlike Dionysus who, when disguised as the Stranger, complies with Pentheus' guards and wins them over, Pentheus' continual efforts to make his authority known undermine his ability to attract others to his cause. Pentheus dies alone and exposed, torn down from his former perch and made an example of human mortality. In large part, Pentheus brings about his own destruction due to his will to stand apart. As will be seen, willingness to admit mortal limitations marks the major difference between Pentheus's fate and that of the third character for discussion: the Bacchae.

III. The Bacchae: Almost Apotheosis

Although made up of numerous individuals, the Bacchae function as one character within the tragedy. The Bacchae act as a group and speak as a group, with the exception of only a few instances where one of them speaks on behalf of the rest. When Dionysus destroys Pentheus' palace the chorus of the tragedy, composed of Asian Bacchae, reacts to Dionysus' earthquake and lightning strike with fear. Their reaction demonstrates the commonality of the group, despite its composition of individuals. The chorus leader cries: "Look how Pentheus' palace will be shaken to its fall" (587). One part of the chorus replies: "Didn't you see the stone lintels reeling... ?" (592). Another part asks: "Don't you see the fire... ?" (596). Each of these three Bacchae speak with one voice and call out to the entire group of Bacchae to ensure that they have all seen the same happening. They all cower together in fear when they experience the earthquake and await the comforting words of the Stranger, who they communally recognize as their leader. The degree of collectivity that exists within the Bacchae's manner of speech and action highlights their function as one character within the tragedy.

Despite the unity of speech and action outlined above, a messenger challenges the commonality of the Bacchae when he reports what he sees of them to Pentheus. He informs Pentheus that "Autonoe was the leader of one group, your mother Agave of another, and Ino of a third" (681). In other words, he expresses that not all of the Bacchae are the same, and that distinctions in rank exist among them. Agave, Autonoe, and Ino used to be royalty in Thebes as Cadmus' daughters, but as bacchants they do not retain such sharp status distinctions. The Bacchae primarily honor Dionysus as exalted, and they collectively find comfort in the Stranger as their representative. Agave, Ino, and Autonoe may be recognized as group leaders among the Bacchae, but their acts of leadership show that such distinctions do not much matter. The actions of the Bacchae always occur synchronously, and no significant individual actions take place among the separate group members. The most pointed act of leadership occurs when Agave shouts to the Bacchae just before the death of Pentheus: "Come, stand round in a circle, maenads, and let us each take hold of a branch so we can capture the mounted beast" (1106). The nature of her order to the other Bacchae is to join together to complete a task. Rather than demanding others to do her bidding, Agave includes herself within the scope of the action. Her actions differ from Pentheus' aforementioned style of leadership, where he delegates tasks to others and pulls away from association with the commoners of Thebes. The differences in leadership style between Agave and Pentheus demonstrate how insignificant the distinctions among the Bacchae are. Unlike Pentheus, Agave is not focused on retaining her individuality or excluding herself from labor; rather, her behavior is inclusive and attests to the commonality of the Bacchae. Even though the messenger points out that there are leaders among the Bacchae, these leaders are not so different from the rest, which lends credence to the Bacchae's identification as one collective unit.

One episode within the tragedy offers a glimpse at the unity present within the Bacchae's social existence on Mount Cithaeron. A messenger gives Pentheus an account of the behavior of the Bacchae. Within the messenger's description, the Bacchae behave well within the bounds of a functional social structure. He states, "Throwing off the fresh sleep from their eyes they sprang to their feet, a miracle of discipline to behold" (692). When he says "miracle of discipline," the messenger means the synchronized actions of the Bacchae, for they all wake simultaneously. These synchronous actions show just how unified the Bacchae are. Without any perceived distinctions among individuals in the group, conflict among those individuals ceases. It appears as though the Bacchae achieve a utopian state of existence, where they coexist with each other and with their environment, each providing for each. The messenger mentions that, "Some, holding in their arms a fawn or wild wolf cubs, offered them white milk – those who had just given birth and whose breasts were still swollen, having left their new-born at home" (699). Every indication suggests that all of the Bacchae would do the same if able, and their peaceful existence in a group setting touches on the limits of commonality. In addition, the messenger describes the earth providing milk for the Bacchae: "As many as had a desire for white drink, scraping through the earth with their sharp fingers they got springing jets of milk" (708). Their existence appears harmonious, yet the social nature of the group disappears. Interaction among the individual bacchants fades into the background and unified group actions take over. These group actions operate without the recognition of the individual and instead only recognize the unified whole. The social utopia that the Bacchae experience approaches the original meaning of the term – a social "nowhere," where society itself disappears into the existence of a Bacchic unit devoid of distinguishable individuals.

The bacchants' loss of individuality becomes more apparent when one considers whether the Bacchae perceive themselves as human or animal. Their culpability to frenzy and nearly irrational rage differs greatly from the ordered social behavior that Pentheus holds to be characteristic of a healthy society. Instead, the Bacchae appear to exist in a natural state without any notable social distinctions. The Bacchae's dismemberment of Pentheus exemplifies their inability to distinguish between men and beasts. The messenger who witnessed the event reports that the Bacchae saw Pentheus as a beast and tore him limb from limb: "One was carrying an arm, another a foot still in its hunting boot. The ribs were laid bare by the tearing apart... the pitiful head... [Agave] carries it, as if it were the head of a mountain lion" (1133). Not only do the Bacchae confuse a man for an animal, but they also tear it to pieces with their hands, thereby avoiding the use of conventional weapons and instead reverting to the bestial behavior of slaughtering prey without any artifice whatsoever. The Bacchae act as beasts rather than humans, yet they do not recognize the nature of their behavior. They exist in a social setting where their individuality ceases and their ability to discern simplifies, allowing them to distinguish only between group-member and outsider.

The Bacchae worship Dionysus by imitating him via the same garb of dappled fawnskin and ivy creepers that Dionysus wears as the Stranger. Their costumes suggest that the Bacchae ultimately desire to achieve complete, lasting union with the god. Throughout Euripides' *Bacchae*, dressing up in the vestments of Dionysus shows him reverence and respect. The chorus of Bacchae calls Thebes to dress up in the god: "crown yourself with ivy! Abound Abound, with rich berry-laden evergreen creepers!" (106). Cadmus and Tiresias wear "the trappings of the god" to exalt Dionysus' greatness (180). When the Bacchae adorn themselves with ivy and don their dappled fawnskins, they abandon their individuality in order to embrace a sense of commonality with Dionysus. They imitate him to become one with him. The Bacchae worship a god who "introduced [wine] to mortals to stop their sorrow and pain" (279). They also indulge in the intoxication of wine and dancing in hopes to find lasting union with Dionysus. However, the Bacchae merely put on the costume of the god, and cannot truly become him. Their efforts only allow them to escape human suffering temporarily. Even though they appear completely willing to abandon their identities, the Bacchae are unable to shed their mortality and truly become Dionysus. This inability reveals a limitation in the potential success of the imitative process: permanently and completely parting with individual identity cannot transform an individual beyond the limitations of their mortal frame. Unlike Pentheus, the Bacchae are willing to abandon their identities to achieve their desire. Just as with Pentheus, however, the Bacchae want more than they are able to achieve, and imitation cannot permanently grant them the virtues of something they are not. Pentheus cannot become a bacchant, and the Bacchae cannot become Dionysus.

As was mentioned, an important distinction between the fates of Pentheus and the Bacchae is that the Bacchae are partially able to fulfill their desires, whereas Pentheus is not. One reason for this difference is that the Bacchae receive the god's aid throughout the course of the tragedy. Dionysus responds to the prayers of the Bacchae. He ultimately allows them to succeed in defeating Pentheus and to achieve the freedom to worship without persecution. In addition, Dionysus allows the Bacchae temporary relief from the suffering of mortal existence by possessing them. The Bacchae experience states of frenzy which eliminate their ability to distinguish much at all, and their utopian mode of existence in the forest is as good a consolation as any for their inability to achieve permanent union with Dionysus. At times, the distinction between the Bacchae and their god becomes very slight, such as when the Bacchae enter into a frenzy which renders them impervious to the weapons of the Theban soldiers. A messenger reports, "The men's sharp-pointed spears drew no blood from the maenads, neither bronze nor iron" (761). In this instance, the Bacchae embody the terrifying aspect of Dionysus that Tiresias outlines earlier in the play. Tiresias tells Pentheus: "[Dionysus] also shares some of Ares' bellicose spirit; for fear sends panic through a marching militia... before it ever even touches the spear" (302). Dionysus and the Bacchae come into very close contact at several points within the tragedy; however, the unity they experience is only temporary. Even though Dionysus does not allow the Bacchae to achieve complete or permanent union with him, he grants them the next best thing: momentary union.

At first glance, the cooperation of the god seems to be an unfair and arbitrary advantage that the Bacchae have over Pentheus. However, the Bacchae ask for Dionysus' help throughout the play. As opposed to Pentheus' misunderstanding of self-limitations, the Bacchae understand that they require aid from external sources to fulfill their desire. The Bacchae cry: "Son of Zeus, Dionysus, do you see this, how your proclaimers struggle against oppression? Come down from Mt. Olympus, lord" (550). In this instance the Bacchae admit their inability to solve their own problems. Their somber plea highlights that the Bacchae understand how human they are, despite their wish to be otherwise. The understanding of self-limitations marks a significant difference between the Bacchae and Pentheus because both characters are human. The Bacchae comprise a group of mortals who collectively imitate Dionysus. However, their failure to do so does not put them in extreme danger, for even though the Bacchae cannot become gods, it is plausible that they would overpower Pentheus by means of their numbers alone. Even so, the Bacchae receive cooperation from Dionysus, which makes quick work of Pentheus' undoing. The messenger who describes how the Bacchae killed Pentheus says that, "the god gave a special ease to [their] hands" (1128). Pentheus faces much higher risk when he attempts to imitate the Bacchae. Not only does Pentheus underestimate the dangers of one versus many, but he also disregards his messenger's previous account of the ferocity of the women on the mountain. Pentheus rejects Dionysus' divinity and falsely assumes that he can succeed upon his own powers. The refusal to compromise, the overestimation of his abilities, and the underestimation of his enemies lead Pentheus to disaster. By contrast, the willingness to call for aid and the knowledge of self-limitations allow the Bacchae to achieve their desire, at least partially. Even though Dionysus sides with the Bacchae, Pentheus' inflated belief in his capabilities leads him to make the hubristic and imprudent decisions that lead to his destruction.

Dionysus, Pentheus, and the Bacchae all have distinct desires within Euripides' tragedy, yet they all attempt to fulfill them through imitation. Dionysus assumes a mortal form to reveal his godhead to Thebes without destroying it. He takes on the characteristics of a human at the expense of appearing like a god. However, since he is a god, Dionysus can simultaneously interact with mortals in a human form and appear in distinctly godlike manifestations. Because of this ability, Dionysus succeeds in fulfilling his desire. Pentheus attempts to imitate a bacchant to spy on the Bacchae, which he ultimately hopes will facilitate the attainment of his desire to earn Thebes' respect as a leader. He becomes less and less like himself in the process, but ultimately fails: he cannot shed his individuality to the extent he needs to become one of the Bacchae, and is instead torn apart at their hands. The Bacchae attempt to become one with Dionysus by dressing up in his vestments. They hope to abandon their identities completely and experience lasting oneness with the god. Yet their mortal nature prevents this from happening, and at most the Bacchae experience temporary unity with Dionysus. Donning the dappled fawnskin, although it allows each character to distance themselves from their identities, cannot permanently alter those identities. For Dionysus this is not a problem, since he ultimately wants to be recognized a god. However, both the Bacchae and

Pentheus suffer because of their inability to assume new identities through imitation. The fates of these characters show that mortals, although unable to resolve the tension between individuality and commonality, can still cope with it, if willing. If not, such mortals may very well be torn apart by that tension.